THE KEW GARDENER'S GUIDE TO

GROWING
HOUSE
PLANTS

Royal Botanic Gardens Kew

THE KEW GARDENER'S GUIDE TO

GROWING HOUSE PLANTS

THE ART AND SCIENCE TO GROW YOUR OWN HOUSE PLANTS

KAY MAGUIRE

WHITE LION
PUBLISHING

Contents

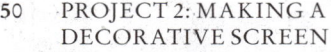

Introduction to growing house plants

—

THE VALUE OF HOUSE PLANTS

People have been growing plants in their homes for thousands of years. From the ancient Egyptians to the Victorians, from palms to cast-iron plants, plants have been used in the home for food, perfume, health or simply for the beauty they bring. The fashion and passion for them have fluctuated over the years, but they always prevail and are currently experiencing a revival.

One of the primary reasons we grow house plants is for their sheer splendour and for what they can bring to our homes. Many house plants are evergreen, chosen for their lush foliage colours, textures and shapes, while flowering plants add vibrant colour and often delicious scent. Increasingly, they are justifiably recognized as design features in their own right, and today there is more choice than ever.

Plants are also good for our health – both mental and physical. It has long been known that plants have a positive effect in the workplace and they are just as effective in the home. Psychologically, simply looking at plants lifts our mood. We respond to them in an instinctive way – looking at plants is just as restful whether they are inside the house or out in the garden. The close connection with nature has a beneficial effect plus caring after something is therapeutic.

House plants give those with no outdoor space the chance to nurture plants but, unlike a garden, house plants can accompany us wherever we live and move to, growing and maturing with us through the years.

Institutions such as the National Aeronautics and Space Administration (NASA) have studied individual plants and noted that they are actively good for our health, cleaning the air of pollutants and volatile organic compounds – many of them ingredients in everyday cleaning products or paints – by filtering them through leaves and roots (see also Natural air fresheners, page 124).

There are plants to suit every spot and every room, from the slowest-growing, most undemanding cacti to the more needy, tropical plants. This book explains the many different types and requirements of house plants and helps you identify those that will grow best in your home. It gives you the inspiration and help to get started and continue to keep your house plants happy and in the very best of health.

Whichever house plants you chose to grow, they will bring colour, interest and clean air to your home or office.

WHAT CAN WE GROW AND WHERE?

The house plants we grow come from a huge range of habitats and ecologies around the world. They are at home on the rainforest floor or high on a mountaintop; they can survive in the bleakest deserts and the wettest swamps, and it is these conditions we need to emulate at home if the plants are to thrive.

Knowing where your plant comes from is the first step in getting it right. Start by understanding the life your plant enjoys in its natural habitat; picture its native environment and you will know exactly what you need to give it to keep it happy.

House plants tend to fall into eight main groups. Although there are some differences within each group, they generally have very distinct requirements reflective of where they come from in the wild.

Ferns

These beautiful foliage plants have many different leaf, or frond, shapes and textures. They range from the spectacular to the delicate and graceful, but all thrive in the world's forests and woodlands and have been around for thousands of years.

They flourish on the damp, shady forest floor where conditions are humid and sunlight is filtered through the taller plants growing above. Replicate this at home with a warm, humid spot out of direct light.

Ferns do not bear flowers or seeds but reproduce by tiny spores held in sporangia, which can sometimes be seen as brown markings on the undersides of the leaves. Ferns must not dry out – keep them moist in your most humid room or mist every day.

Palms

Elegant, stately and architectural, with arching stems and decorative, fan-shaped fronds, palms are the plants for creating a jungle in your home. They are the perfect statement plants.

Hailing from the subtropics and tropics, palms are at home in habitats as diverse as rainforests and deserts, but all like warmth and good light – the leaf shape is specifically designed to catch the light. They appreciate humidity, so mist them in spring and summer and keep moist, watering them regularly, as soon as the top of the compost starts to feel dry. Clean their fronds by standing them under a tepid shower or outside when summer rains are forecast. Many palms are also very good for the indoor environment, as their leaves absorb toxins and cleanse the air we breathe (see also Natural air fresheners, page 124).

Succulents

Drought-loving plants, grown mainly for their stunning shapes, textures and foliage, succulents are a huge group (which includes cacti) and can be tiny, fleshy rosettes or huge, spiky 'trees'. Some are trailing, others shrub-like and many have brilliantly coloured flowers.

Their natural habitats are deserts, mountainous regions and savannah – all areas with low moisture, dry air and warm, bright sunshine. Succulents have evolved into water-storage organs holding moisture in their leaves, stems and tuberous roots, so that they can survive arid conditions. Their leaves, and sometimes stems, are fleshy and

House plants come in a whole host of shapes, textures and leaf colours to make eye-catching features in the home.

often silver or glaucous green, to reflect light. Some have fine hairs on the leaves, too, to trap moisture. They are undemanding plants that love a warm, bright spot, and are some of the very few plants to cope with baking heat and sunshine.

Mimic their natural ecology by planting them in an open, free-draining compost mix (see page 22). Always let water drain away after watering. The simplest way to make sure succulents are not sitting in soggy soil is to water from below (see page 23). Water well during the growing season, but then let them rest – watering only once the compost has dried out.

Cacti
From the dramatic, sculptural and spiky to the fluffy and weird, cacti are another large group of plants. Although a type of succulent, many have adapted to life in the deserts of the world by modifying their leaves into spines and their stems into plump water-storage organs, to help them through arid times. They love warm, dry air, bright sunshine and free, open soil. Others hail from woodlands and prefer shade and humidity, so always check their cultural needs when you buy them.

Desert cacti are used to waiting a long time for water, so never overwater; let the compost dry out before watering again and give them a rest in winter. Cacti like warm days and cool nights so a bright windowsill is perfect – just make sure it is not too hot in summer. These easy plants are ideal for less green-fingered growers.

Bromeliads and air plants
Glamorous and exotic-looking bromeliads are epiphytes – plants that grow on trees and shrubs without doing any harm, and getting their water and nutrients from the rain and atmosphere. Tropical bromeliads each form a rosette of leaves with a central well that, in the wild, collects water and forest debris funnelled down from the leaves. This is then broken down by the plant and used as food. Many have stripy or colourful leaves, and once mature they produce striking

spikes of bright, colourful bracts with tiny flowers within, which can last for months. After flowering, bromeliads die, but they do produce baby offsets (called pups) at the bases of their leaves. These are easily removed and grown on into new plants (see page 32).

Air plants are some of easiest plants to grow, coping with neglect and capable of growing without soil. Native to the Americas in habitats that range from swampy forests to bleak mountaintops, they need indirect light and a soak in water once a week. They can rot if kept too wet so shake well and hang upside down to dry (see also Driftwood anchor, page 134).

Air plants are good for the bedroom, releasing oxygen at night rather than in the day and improving the air quality we breathe while asleep.

Flowering plants

Flowering plants introduce colour and cheer quite unlike the drama and tapestry of green that foliage plants produce. They include trailing and climbing plants, bulbs and plants with some of the most intoxicating fragrances that add yet another dimension to a display.

Such plants can be temperamental as you are promoting flowers as well as good health, and some may need a cool period to encourage blooms.

Foliage plants

Leafy plants with insignificant flowers are grown for their stunning foliage shapes, textures, colour or variegation. Many make wonderful design features in a room, and their lush, green leaves create an oasis of calm. This group includes some of the easiest and most indestructible plants – perfect for first-time or nervous growers.

Usually from the tropical rainforests or woodlands, they need moist potting compost and high humidity, and most tolerate low light levels.

Carnivorous plants

These amazing plants have adapted to life in the nutrient-poor peat bogs of the wild by cunningly turning their leaves into traps that catch insects and other small creatures. Some have leaves that have evolved into long,

deep pitchers; others produce leaves dripping in sticky drops that curl around their prey, while the 'jaws' of the ever-popular Venus fly trap (see page 64) snap tight over any insect that lands on it. Once caught, enzymes break down the insect so that the plant can absorb its nutrients.

Carnivorous plants have very specific needs. Most require bright light and a permanently boggy compost mix kept damp with rainwater.

HOW TO GROW HOUSE PLANTS

House plants are available from specialist shops, nurseries, garden centres, supermarkets and online, but before you shop observe and assess your home so that you know what kind of conditions each room can offer.

Once you have found a plant to meet the appropriate conditions, check it over to make sure it is perky (not wilting) and in the best condition. Go for plants that have an even, bushy shape and healthy foliage with no yellowing, browning or disease on leaves and stems. Check the compost for pests, and lift the plant from its pot to see if the roots are congested – if they are, choose another or repot it when you get home. Finally, ensure the plant is wrapped and protected against the weather or damage on the way home.

Once home, unwrap new plants and repot them if they needed – especially if they are in pots without drainage holes. If the soil is dry, give a good water and leave to drain.

Finding the right spot

Every house plant needs light, water and warmth. Your job is to provide

OPPOSITE FAR LEFT A group of lush foliage plants creates a vibrant green feature and instils a feeling of calm.
OPPOSITE ABOVE Enchanting and exotic, air plants are some of the easiest plants to grow in our homes.
OPPOSITE BELOW House plants that produce flowers, such as the dainty African violet, bring another dimension to a display.

Many forms of succulents and cacti thrive in the baking heat of a sunny window. Here are examples of *Pilosocereus* (left), *Echeveria* (top centre) and *Haworthia* (bottom centre).

similar conditions – as close as possible – to its native habitat. If you give each house plant the apropriate place it will thrive – its new home must be the right place for it and not you!

Many plants, particularly tropical ones, need a settling-in period and may struggle at first, but this is to be expected. Resist the urge to keep moving plants to potentially better spots; give them time to find their 'feet'.

Light
This is a crucial source of energy for all plants. Although the amount of light an individual plant needs varies, all plants require some during the day.

The majority of plants we grow in our homes need bright, indirect light rather than direct sunlight, but there are plenty that prefer a shadier spot.

The amount of light a room receives depends on the size of the windows, whether the light source is direct or indirect, and the aspect – south-facing windows are the brightest, then east-, then west-, with north-facing ones receiving little sun at all.

The area directly in front of a south-facing window usually gets the strongest and most direct light. In summer, particularly, this will be too much for almost all plants except the toughest cacti and succulents.

ABOVE, LEFT AND BELOW The many different types of house plants each need their own particular spot to thrive, be it within the humidity of a group, mimicking the conditions of the rainforest or basking in full sun as they would on the desert floor. Remember that both the light and temperature in your home need to be taken into account.

Bright, indirect light is found in front of west- and east-facing windows and a couple of metres/yards back from a south-facing one.

Semi-shade occurs in front of a north-facing window or to the side of one in a brighter room. The darkest, shadiest spots are in the back and sides of a room, particularly in rooms that receive no direct light or light for just a short time, although bright walls and mirrors help to reflect light in a room.

Light levels are reduced the closer you get to the ceiling, so remember this when choosing plants for hanging baskets, top shelves or on cupboards (see also Hanging gardens, page 84).

Remember that light is stronger in summer than in winter, so move plants that prefer brighter conditions nearer a window in the gloomier months.

If you can, turn plants every few days, so that they get even amounts of light and grow straight and balanced. Also, keep leaves clean – too much dust can prevent leaves absorbing light.

Temperature

Almost all house plants like temperatures that are warm during the day and cooler at night. Some such as tropical plants want a hotter spot, while others such as palms and carnivorous plants prefer life a little cooler. However, none likes dramatic swings of hot or cold, so avoid any draughts near doors and windowsills (where temperatures will drop considerably at night behind curtains) and keep plants away from ovens, radiators, fires and heaters. Note that some plants may need a cooler winter temperature, to promote flowering.

Humidity

Many plants, particularly those from the tropics, require a warm, moist atmosphere, with vapour levels in the air that are much higher than we can achieve normally in our centrally heated homes. Without the appropriate humidity level, plant leaves shrivel, turn brown and drop off, and growth can be stunted. Steamy bathrooms and kitchens are the obvious choice for plants such as these, but if you want to grow them elsewhere see page 25 for tips on how to raise humidity.

HOW TO DISPLAY YOUR HOUSE PLANTS

House plants are increasingly considered an integral part of a room's style and, just as a sculpture or painting might be used, plants are often viewed as design features in their own right. They can set the mood of a room, adding a sense of calm or bringing drama and excitement.

Depending on their size and look, plants can be positioned on their own as focal points within a room or be displayed together in contrasting or harmonizing groups. Collections can be used to divide a room or create screens for privacy (see Making a decorative screen, page 50), while hanging and trailing plants can draw the eye upwards in a small, cramped room, making it appear bigger.

You need to consider all aspects of their appearance before you can be sure that you have got their display right.

Shape

Many plants have silhouettes and shapes that grab our attention, while

Plants that need humidity, such as this Boston fern (*Nephrolepis exaltata*), are an ideal choice for the steamy conditions in a bathroom.

others need to be seen up close to be appreciated. Plants can be tall and straight, rounded or hummock-shaped, and some climb up or trail down loosely. Some shapes work as simple stand-alone, sculptural elements. Others add impact and harmony when grown in groups, creating contrasting or symmetrical patterns depending on their appearance.

Size

The size of your plant affects how it relates to other plants or features in your room. A large, single plant will stand out and draw the eye, but smaller plants look better together. Groups of plants that are the same size or shape use repetition to create a simple, ordered effect, while plants that are of varying heights will bring a more dynamic, natural look.

Texture

Plant textures can range from smooth and glossy to lacy or spiky. As well as bringing visual interest, textures can be tactile, enticing viewers to touch and admire. Using house plants with different or harmonizing textures keeps your display vibrant and interesting.

Cacti and succulents have strong visual textures that can be used

ABOVE AND LEFT Collections of different plants can create a vibrant atmosphere while a single species (such as this heart leaf, left), repeated *en masse* brings a feeling of calm to a room.
BELOW Hanging plants help to draw the eye upwards and can make a small room feel bigger.

repetitively for emphasis or in contrast with other textures to encourage the eye to look at each individual plant.

Once you have assessed a plant's individual design strengths it is time to decide how to use them. The style of pot in which you grow a plant can change its look instantly. Neutral pots enhance a plant's shape, colour and texture and make the plant itself stand out. A bolder or patterned container can complement your plant's texture or highlight different features and attract attention, helping to make the plant a focal point.

ABOVE A few key tools such as secateurs, a hand trowel and a watering can are the most important ones when starting to grow plants at home.

Only when a plant is sited in appropriate growing conditions, so it thrives and is happy, can it become the statement or feature you want it to be.

EQUIPMENT

The range of kit deemed necessary for caring for house plants is sometimes daunting, but in fact you need only a few key tools to get started. Do not scrimp on the essentials – the better the quality tools the longer they will last.

The essentials
- Watering can – one with a long, narrow spout will help you water the base of the plant rather than the leaves. A fine rose will enable you to water plants from above.
- Secateurs or strong scissors – for snipping dead leaves and flowers and for trimming and pruning plants into shape.
- Mister spray – for spritzing plants that need high humidity (see pages 16 and 25).
- Pebbles – in a bowl, saucer or tray to increase humidity levels around your plants.
- Grit or gravel – for mulching plants such as cacti, to help keep moisture away from the stems and leaves.
- Soft cloth – for wiping dust from leaves (see also Natural air fresheners, page 124).
- Small paintbrush – for removing stray compost and dust from prickly- and furry-leaved plants.

- Pots – plastic, terracotta and a collection of decorative ones in a range of materials.
- Pot saucers and trays – for catching water as it drips through the pot's drainage holes and to protect furniture and floor coverings.
- Potting compost – house plants will not survive in ordinary garden soil and many need a specific compost or compost mix to thrive (see opposite).
- Fertilizer – most house plants require an occasional boost with a dilute liquid feed or slow-release fertilizer granules (see page 27).

Useful extras
- Small hand trowel – for scooping compost and gravel and for making planting holes in compost.
- Small hand fork – for loosening potting compost.
- Canes – for supporting plants and for training them in specific directions.
- Twine or string – for tying plants to supports.
- Gloves – for holding prickly plants.
- Tweezers – for cleaning cacti.

Containers
The most important kit is your collection of planting pots. Providing it is big enough, you can use pretty much anything as a container for your plants, depending on the style of your home and the look you are aiming for.

Pots in plastic, terracotta, metal, wood and ceramic are widely available in an array of colours and designs. You can use them as a decorative cover pot (or cachepot) to sit your plastic pot inside or you can pot your plant directly into a decorative container provided that it has drainage holes to allow excess water to drain away.

Do not use too large a new container for your plant. Start your plant off in a decorative pot that is the same size as its original plastic pot or the next size up – just a few centimetres or so bigger in diameter.

POTTING COMPOST
Always use new potting compost to pot up a plant – old compost can contain diseases and will have fewer nutrients. Never use garden soil.

Different house plants have their own compost needs depending on their native environment. Many will be happy in good-quality, multipurpose potting compost, which is the most cost-effective. However, for some types such as cacti and succulents or carnivorous plants, specialist compost mixes are definitely worth the extra cost. You can also make your own.

Making your own compost mixes
You need to add certain materials (described below) to good-quality, peat-free, multipurpose potting compost, in order to create the right drainage and growing environment for individual plants. For the appropriate proportions for each plant type, see Compost mixes, page 22.

- *Grit* (available at garden centres as horticultural grit) is mixed into compost to create free-draining conditions. It can also be used in a layer at the base of a pot (to create

Plants that like free-draining conditions, such as cacti and succulents, will benefit from a compost mix containing an equal amount of grit.

a reservoir that water can drain into) and as a mulch layer on the surface of the compost (to conserve moisture and keep it away from the stems of the plant).

- *Perlite* is a coarse granular mineral; when mixed with compost it improves aeration and provides free-draining conditions.
- *Horticultural sand* is a cleaner, finer sand than builders' sand and is combined with compost to improve drainage.
- *Milled bark* has good water-holding capacity and is increasingly added to peat-free mixes.

Peat-free composts
Peat is a finite natural resource and its extraction from bogs in the wild is destructive – often threatening the habitats of the very plants that we wish to grow at home; it is unsustainable, too, as peat takes hundreds of years to develop and, therefore, replace. Peat also contains few nutrients and is terrible at holding moisture, meaning plants dry out quickly and are difficult to re-wet.

Opt for peat-free composts such as those containing coir. Note that if the manufacturer does not specifically state the contents are peat-free on the bag they will not be.

COMPOST MIXES

Cacti and succulents
Because they come from poor, dry locations these plants need open, gritty soil that lets water flow through freely. Mix an equal amount of multipurpose potting compost with grit, perlite or horticultural sand.

Ferns and tropical plants
Being happy in denser, nutrient-rich, moist soil, these plants will enjoy good-quality, multipurpose potting compost.

Carnivorous plants
These plants live in acidic, nutrient-poor peat bogs in the wild and need permanently wet soil. A traditional carnivorous potting mix would include peat, but many nurseries and growers have successively trialled growing without it. One such carniverous plant grower is Shropshire Sarracenias, which recommends a mix of one part perlite, one part grit and two parts milled bark.

MULCHES

A layer of grit, gravel or small pebbles on the surface of the compost stops moisture rotting the stems and leaves of plants that like dry conditions, such as cacti and succulents.

REPOTTING

At some point your house plants will need potting on into larger pots – either immediately after purchase if their original pots have no drainage holes or their compost is poor or because they have outgrown their current pots.

Most plants are usually ready for a new pot every 2–3 years. Signs that it is getting too big for their pot include roots coming through the holes in the base, a bulging – even splitting – pot, or simply a struggling plant. Remove the plant from its pot and check its root ball to see if it is pot-bound, with congested roots circling round and round the root ball.

The best time to repot is in early spring, just as plants are coming back into active growth. Some, however, may prefer this done after flowering (see individual plant entries, pages 34–141).

Water your plant the day before you plan to repot it. Choose a pot that is only one size larger, about 5cm/2in, than the current one; if the container is too big, your plant will end up sitting in soggy, waterlogged soil. Put the appropriate compost into the base of the pot and, holding your plant carefully around the base of the stem, ease it from its pot, tapping it to loosen it if you need to. Tease out congested roots with your fingers and then place the plant in the new pot, adjusting its height by adding or removing compost until the top of the root ball is about 2cm/¾in from the top of the pot. Fill in around the plant with more compost, firming it in gently as you go and then water in the newly potted plant.

Larger plants can be difficult to remove from their container, so simply topdress these instead. Use a trowel to remove the top 5cm/2in of compost, then sprinkle on slow-release fertilizer granules. Add a fresh layer of compost up to the original compost level, and water to settle it in.

Most plants need repotting once their roots reach the edges of the pot. However, some actively thrive when root-bound so always check first.

WATERING

Watering is your most crucial job when it comes to caring for your house plants, and the ultimate aim is to get to know your plants well enough that you recognize the signs when they require a drink. When you buy a plant always read the label so you know whether it prefers life on the dry or damper side.

Check your plants regularly by feeling the top 5cm/2in of compost with your fingers to see if it is wet or dry. Most house plants like to be kept moist through spring and summer and drier during the cooler, darker months of winter. Very few like to sit in soggy compost, and too much water is far more harmful than too little, causing rotting and fungal diseases. Therefore, always grow plants in pots with plenty of holes so water can drain away. Check them an hour after watering and tip out any excess water that has collected in saucers or decorative pots.

Watering from the top
This method is good for most plants but, to avoid getting water on the leaves or stems, use a can with a long spout and aim it directly at the compost.

Watering from below
Plants that do not like wet leaves or crowns, are wilting or whose leaves are

The benefits of rainwater

Many house plants dislike tap water because it contains fluorides and chloride. Soft water is full of salts while hard water has high levels of calcium, which is unsuitable for ericaceous plants and can also build up and block plant pores. Rainwater is the ideal alternative, but it is difficult to get hold of unless you have the time and space to collect it outside. Do, if you can, particularly if growing carnivorous or air plants, which really prefer it. Otherwise, use tap water but flush plants through with rainwater or bottled water every couple of months.

You can also use bottled or filtered water to water house plants, but this is expensive, or simply boil tap water and use it once it has cooled.

covering the compost are best watered from below. Put your plant on a saucer and fill it with water. Allow the plant to suck up as much water as it needs for around 15 minutes and then remove it from the saucer and let it drain.

Watering from above the plant with a can with a fine rose

For plants that like being drenched, such as many tropical plants and ferns, hold the can above the foliage when watering.

Watering a bromeliad

These plants each form a rosette of leaves with a central well that collects rainwater in the wild. On your house plant this needs to be kept topped up.

However, every month you should empty it and refill it with fresh water, to stop the water stagnating.

Air plants can be misted a couple of times a week or simply soaked in a sink of tepid water once a week for an hour. Just make sure you shake off any excess moisture, which will rot the leaves. Always use rainwater if you can (see also Driftwood anchor, page 134).

How to revive a forgotten plant

If a plant is wilting and its compost is bone dry, immerse the entire root ball in a bucket or sink of water for 30 minutes. You may need to hold it in the water to stop it bobbing up. If the compost is struggling to re-wet, add just a drop of washing-up liquid, which should help the compost absorb the water.

HOLIDAY CARE

Going away can be difficult when you have a house plant collection, but ideally friends and family will drop by to water and keep an eye on them. If you cannot rely on others, here are some simple tricks to ensure your plants stay hydrated and happy while you are away.

Water your plants well before you go and then place them somewhere that is not too warm and out of direct light. Grouping them together will increase the humidity around them and stop them drying out too quickly. If you have plants that need high humidity levels, fill a bowl with pebbles and water and place it in the centre of the group.

Another way to stop house plants drying out is to fill the kitchen sink with water. Then lay an absorbent cloth such as a tea towel across the draining board, leaving one end hanging over the edge

An atomizer, or mister, will spritz water into the air around your plants, such as this mosaic plant, raising the humidity levels in a warm, dry room.

into the water. Group your plants on top of the cloth. While you are away, the cloth will slowly soak up water, which your plants will then absorb, drawing it up into the compost.

To water individual plants while you are away on holiday, cut the base off an old plastic water bottle and make a hole in the lid. Position the bottle lid well into the compost and then pour water into the bottle. This will slowly seep into the compost, keeping it moist.

RAISING HUMIDITY

House plants from the warm, moist tropics like a damp, humid atmosphere (see page 16). A steamy bathroom or kitchen is perfect for them. Increase the humidity around them by growing them together in groups, by spritzing plants with water every day using a mister spray or by placing them on or next to a saucer or bowl filled with pebbles and water.

TEMPERATURE

Most house plants tolerate a broad temperature range so for their optimum growth you just have to ensure that the conditions in their vicinity stay within that range; otherwise, plants will start to struggle.

What plants really dislike are wild fluctuations in temperature and

ABOVE AND LEFT House plants spend their entire lives in containers and so need help from us to thrive. Feeding them regularly provides the nutrients they require to ensure healthy leaves and flowers, here on a Natal lily).
BELOW Nip out any dead leaves (here on a geranium) to prevent disease and to keep plants looking good.

extremes of hot or cold. No plants should have to cope with the blasting, drying heat from a radiator or fire. Plants also hate the sudden drop in temperature that occurs on a windowsill behind closed curtains at night. Draughty spots in halls and doorways are no-go areas, too.

Finally, remember that heat rises, which means that plants in hanging baskets and on top shelves will dry out quicker than house plants down on the floor or on a table.

FEEDING

Unlike plants growing outside in the ground, house plants are cultivated permanently in pots and are entirely dependent on us for their food and water supplies.

Potting composts contain a finite amount of nutrients that will feed your plants for the first six or so weeks after planting. After this it is up to you to help them thrive by giving them extra food through the growing season.

Most foliage plants just need a general balanced fertilizer, but certain types of plants such as cacti and orchids should be given specialist house-plant fertilizers. High-potash ones are useful for promoting flowering in house plants grown for their blooms.

Feed plants only when they are actively growing between spring

and autumn, and always follow the manufacturer's instructions, resisting the temptation to overdose.

Liquid fertilizers are a great way to give plants a quick boost as they are easy to apply and immediately absorbed. They are available either as liquid or powders that are mixed with water or as a ready-to-go liquid.

Slow-release fertilizers gradually provide nutrients to the plant and are available as granules or sticks that are scattered over or pushed into the potting compost.

CLEANING

Inevitably, dust builds up on plant leaves, making them look grubby. It also stops light getting to the leaves and blocks their pores (see also Natural air fresheners, page 124).

Use a soft, damp cloth to gently clean large, glossy leaves; avoid house plant polish, which will clog the leaf pores. For plants with furry or prickly leaves, rub the foliage gently with a soft brush or a cotton bud, and use tweezers to pick out lumps of compost or gravel. Plants with lots of narrow leaves such as palms can be stood under the shower – just take care not to drown them.

If leaves or flowers die back, nip them out with sharp scissors or secateurs so that they do not cause rotting or harbour pests and diseases.

Regularly cleaning house plant leaves with a soft, damp cloth helps to keep them dust-free and allows light to get to the leaf pores.

PROPAGATION BY LEAF CUTTINGS

New house plants can be expensive but many of them are easy to propagate for new plants for you and your friends. This is best done in spring and summer, in water (see Windowsill propagation, page 96) or in cuttings compost. Different types of plants are propagated slightly differently, but they all involve growing a new plant from a single leaf or a section of one.

Snake plant leaf cuttings

You will need:
Seed tray or pot
Cuttings compost mixed with an equal
    amount of perlite
Clean, sharp knife
Clear polythene bag and rubber band

- Water the parent plant half an hour before you are ready to take a cutting.
- Fill a seed tray or pot with the compost mix, then firm to remove air pockets.

Plants for leaf cuttings include:

African violet (*Saintpaulia*)
Cape primrose (*Streptocarpus*)
Flower-dust plant
    (*Kalanchoe pumila*)
Jade plant (*Crassula ovata*)
Moulded-wax succulent
    (*Echeveria agavoides*)
Painted-leaf begonia (*Begonia*)
Radiator plant
    (*Peperomia caperata*)
Snake plant
    (*Sansevieria trifasciata*)

- Choose a young, healthy leaf and use a sharp knife to remove it at the base.
- Cut the leaf horizontally into sections about 5cm/2in wide, making a small notch in the base of each. The notch will ensure you know which part is the base, as cuttings need to be planted in the direction they were growing, and not upside down.
- Plant each leaf cutting, pushing the edge with the notch gently into the compost.
- Carefully water in the cutting with a fine rose on your can; allow the water to drain away.
- Wrap a polythene bag around the pot and seal it with the rubber band; this will raise the humidity and stop the cuttings drying out.
- Place the pot in a warm spot but out of direct sun. The cuttings should root in about six weeks and new plants grow.

PROPAGATION BY STEM CUTTINGS

This is one of the easiest ways to propagate new plants using young, supple growth in spring. While some plants are happy to root in compost, others root just as easily in a glass of water.

Silver-inch plant stem cuttings propagated in water

You will need:
Clean, sharp knife or secateurs
Small glass of water
Small pot
Multipurpose potting compost

When silver-inch plant stems are placed in a glass of water they will start to develop roots in just a few weeks.

- Choose a healthy stem that is not flowering and cut it off at the base.
- Trim any small leaves from the base, making sure there is at least 2cm/¾in of clear stem remaining.
- Place the stem in the glass of water so that no leaves are under the water.
- Leave in a bright spot out of direct sun for a few weeks while roots grow from the base of the stem cuttings.
- Once rooted, transplant the cutting into a small pot of compost and grow on somewhere warm and bright.

Silver-inch plant stem cuttings propagated in compost

You will need:
Clean, sharp knife or secateurs
Seed tray or pot
Multipurpose potting compost mixed
    with an equal amount of perlite
Hormone rooting powder (optional)
Pencil or dibber
Clear polythene bag and rubber band

- Choose a healthy stem that is not flowering and cut it off at the base.
- Trim it to at least 10cm/4in long, just below a leaf joint. Then remove the lower leaves.

The stiff, sharp leaves of snake plant or mother-in-law's tongue arise from a fleshy, underground rhizome. Pieces of rhizome with one leaf can be detached to form new plants.

- Fill a seed tray or pot with the compost mix and water until moist.
- If using hormone rooting powder to speed up rooting, dip the stem cutting into it.
- Use a pencil or dibber to make a hole in the compost and insert your cutting into the hole. Fill in with compost around the stem.
- Cover the seed tray or pot with a plastic bag and seal with the rubber band, to keep the humidity high.
- Keep the compost moist until new shoots appear, then transplant the cutting into a pot and place in a bright spot to grow on.

Plants for stem cuttings include:

African violet (*Saintpaulia*)
Devil's ivy
   (*Epipremnum aureum*)
Missionary plant
   (*Pilea peperomioides*)
Most soft-stemmed plants
Painted-leaf begonia (*Begonia*)
Peacock plant
   (*Goeppertia makoyana*)
Radiator plant
   (*Peperomia caperata*)
Silver-inch plant
   (*Tradescantia zebrina*)

PROPAGATION BY DIVISION

Many clump-forming tropical plants produce new stems around their bases, and these can simply be split with their roots from the parent plants and potted up. This will often give the parent plant a new lease of life, too. Divide plants in spring or after they have finished flowering.

Dividing a plant

You will need:
Newspaper
Clean, sharp knife
Multipurpose potting compost
Pots

Plants for division include:

Asparagus fern
    (*Asparagus setaceus*)
Boston fern
    (*Nephrolepis exaltata*)
Cast-iron plant
    (*Aspidistra elatior*)
False shamrock
    (*Oxalis triangularis*)
Palms such as bamboo palm
    (*Rhapis excelsa*) and parlour
    palm (*Chamaedorea elegans*)
Peace lily
    (*Spathiphyllum wallisii*)
Peacock plant
    (*Goeppertia makoyana*)
Snake plant
    (*Sansevieria trifasciata*)
Some succulents with separate
    stems such as jade plant
    (*Crassula ovata*)
Spineless yukka
    (*Yucca elephantipes*)

- This is an easy but messy job, so lay newspaper down before you start.
- Remove the plant from its pot, lay it on its side and feel around the base and roots with your fingers to find where you can split the plant.
- Separate clumps by gently pulling the plant apart, making sure that each piece has roots attached.
- If the roots are tangled and tricky to extract, use a knife to slice them apart.
- Repot each new section into a pot that is large enough for the roots plus a little room to grow.

PROPAGATION BY OFFSETS

Some plants grow offsets or baby plantlets known as 'pups' around the base of each stem or on the end of long runners that sprout from the plant. Some of these replace the parent plant, which dies after flowering.

Offsets and runners are easy to propagate – just do not be over-eager to remove the baby plants too soon. Always wait until they are large enough and strong enough to survive independently. Ideally, they should be between one- and two-thirds the size of the parent plant.

Propagating offsets

You will need:
Gloves or newspaper if you are
    removing prickly cacti plantlets
Clean, sharp knife
Hormone rooting powder
Small pot
Potting compost appropriate to the
    plant (see page 20)

- Wearing gloves or holding the plant with newspaper, if necessary, gently ease the offset, along with any roots, from the parent plant. Use a knife if it does not pull away easily.
- Dust the offset with hormone rooting powder if the offset does not have roots.
- Plant into a pot of moist, free-draining compost and grow on somewhere warm and light.
- Pot on when new shoots appear.

Propagating offsets on runners:

You will need:
Small pot
Potting compost appropriate to the plant (see page 20)
Clean, sharp knife

Plants with offsets or runners include:

Barbados aloe (*Aloe vera*) – offsets
Bromeliads and air plants – offsets
Donkey's tail (*Sedum morganianum*) – offsets
Many cacti and succulents – offsets
Spider plant (*Chlorophytum comosum* 'Variegatum') – runners

- Choose a plantlet that has a number of leaves and roots growing from the base.
- Fill a small pot with compost and insert the plantlet, taking care not to plant it too deeply. Water in
- Keep the compost moist.
- When new shoots appear, cut the plantlet from the parent plant.

PROPAGATION BY ADVENTITIOUS ROOTS

Climbing plants and some succulents such as donkey's tail (see page 13) produce adventitious roots on their stems. You can cut off a stem section (as described below) or pin them down in compost and grow them on until they can be removed from the parent plant (as with spider plant; see page 57)

Propagating donkey's tail with adventitious roots

You will need:
Clean, sharp knife
Small pot
Potting compost appropriate to the plant (see page 20)

- Use the knife to remove a section of stem with roots.
- Fill a small pot with compost.
- Plant the section into it, firming the roots in gently.
- Water, to settle the compost around the plant.
- Grow on in the warmth and light.

LEFT Many succulents and cacti produce little offsets around their base. These can simply be removed and grown on into new plants.
RIGHT Some succulents produce aerial roots on older stems: these can be detached and potted up.

Plants

Delta maidenhair fern

Adiantum raddianum

These delicate, lacy plants that hail from the humid, shady forests of tropical America are the perfect bathroom plant, thriving in the steamy air. Look out for *A. raddianum* 'Fragrantissimum', with its lush, sweetly scented foliage, and the filigree *A.r.* 'Micropinnulum'.

—

WHERE TO GROW

The graceful, drooping fronds make delta maidenhair fern a lovely choice for a shelf, basket or plant stand in a humid kitchen or bathroom; it also loves the humid atmosphere of a tropical terrarium (see Miniature rainforest, page 118).

HOW TO GROW

Use loam-based compost, which holds moisture better than multipurpose compost. Water the plant at its base. Mist regularly or place the pot on a tray of pebbles and water. Feed once a month from spring to autumn, with a balanced liquid fertilizer. Watering can be reduced in winter but keep humidity levels up. Remove scruffy growth at the base.

GROWING TIP

These are high-maintenance, fussy plants that hate being moved, so give them the perfect spot from the start as they dislike draughts and the blasting heat from radiators.

ALL IN THE MIND
The shiny, black stems on this fern give it its common name as they are thought to resemble human hair.

Family Pteridaceae	
Temperature 10–24°C/50–75°F	
Light Indirect light/ semi-shade	
Water Constantly moist but well-drained	
Height and spread 50x80cm/20x32in	

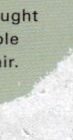

Urn plant

Aechmea fasciata aka silver vase, scarlet star

Elegant, arching leaves are mottled with silver, and in summer the urn plant produces a single flower spike with pale pink bracts and small, but eye-catching, violet flowers. This rainforest plant is easy to look after.

—

WHERE TO GROW
Its beautiful flower spike and striking leaves make this a perfect centrepiece or feature plant on a table or shelf away from a window.

HOW TO GROW
Plant in a 50:50 mix of orchid compost and multipurpose compost. Simply top up the central well with water so that it is always at least 2cm/¾in full. Use rain-, filtered or distilled water. In the growing season, feed every couple of weeks with a diluted liquid fertilizer watered into the well. Let the compost dry out between watering in winter.

GROWING TIP
Although the flower is long-lasting, the urn plant flowers only once and then dies. However, baby offsets are produced at the base after flowering, and once these reach about 10cm/4in they can be propagated (see page 31). New plants take around five years to flower.

Family Bromeliaceae

Temperature
15–25°C/59–77°F

Light Bright but indirect light

Water Water the central well and keep compost moist

Height and spread
60x60cm/24x24in

REGULAR CHANGE
Empty the central well every month and refill, to prevent the water becoming stagnant.

Black aeonium

Aeonium 'Zwartkop' aka black rose

Black aeoniums love a Mediterranean climate that is not too hot, cold, wet or dry. A branching shrub, it has stunning rosettes of purple, almost black, fleshy leaves and in spring diminutive, yellow, star-like flowers. Leaves may go green in winter when the light levels drop, but they will soon colour up as the days get brighter in spring.

WHERE TO GROW
Place on a windowsill from autumn to spring, but move out of direct sun in summer.

HOW TO GROW
Grow in very gritty, free-draining compost. In summer, high temperatures can make them dormant so keep plants almost dry; in other seasons, water when the compost feels dry. Feed monthly in winter with a diluted liquid fertilizer. Black aeonium dies after flowering, but a new plant will grow to replace it.

GROWING TIP
Easily propagated by snipping off a rosette with a few centimetres of stem. Let it dry out for a couple of days and then pot it up; the new plant will root quickly.

Family Crassulaceae

Temperature 10–24°C/50–75°F

Light Sunny/indirect bright light

Water Sparingly; allow plants to dry out between watering

Height and spread 60x60cm/24x24in

SUMMER TREAT
Black aeoniums can be placed outside on a sunny patio or terrace in the garden in summer.

Chinese evergreen

Aglaonema commutatum

These are tough, easy plants that just need warmth and moisture to thrive. Their upright, dark green leaves are marbled with silver, and they make elegant centrepiece plants.

WHERE TO GROW
Chinese evergreen is tolerant of temperature change, provided that life does not get too cool, and so is ideal in a gloomy hall or at the back of a room.

HOW TO GROW
A humid atmosphere is important so mist your plant a couple of times a week or place it on a tray of wet pebbles if growing in a warm room. Feed twice a month from spring to autumn. Nip off any flowers that appear so that energy is concentrated in the leaves. Cut back tatty leaves in spring.

GROWING TIP
Repot plants every couple of years in spring into a slightly larger pot.

Family Araceae

Temperature
16–25˚C/ 61–77˚F

Light Indirect light and shade

Water Let the top 2cm/¾in of compost dry out before watering

Height and spread
45x45cm/18x18in

VIVID CHOICES
Look out for the new hybrids with their red, pink or peach colouring, such as *Aglaonema* 'Pink Dalmatian'. They do, however, need a brighter spot, as too much shade makes their colours fade.

Several steps up

Stepladders are a simple and stylish way to display plants, and the taller they are the more plants you can show off. Make use of the different heights by placing a range of textures and leaf shapes where they can be grown best. Position the softer-leaved, friendlier plants such as ferns, asparagus fern and spider plants where they can be touched and where it does not matter if they are gently brushed against. Place more fragile or spikier specimens higher up.

—

PLANTS FOR THE LOWER SHELVES
Asparagus fern (*Asparagus setaceus*)
Boston fern (*Nephrolepis exaltata*)
Button fern (*Pellaea rotundifolia*)
Cretan brake fern (*Pteris cretica*)
Delta maidenhair fern (*Adiantum raddianum*)
Foxtail fern (*Asparagus densiflorus*)
Spider plant (*Chlorophytum comosum* 'Variegatum')

—

PLANTS FOR THE TOP SHELVES
Barbados aloe (*Aloe vera*)
Black aeonium (*Aeonium* 'Zwartkop')
Bunny-ears cactus (*Opuntia microdasys*)
Golden barrel cactus (*Echinocactus grusonii*)
Old man cactus (*Cephalocereus senilis*)
Pincushion cactus (*Mammillaria*)
Pineapple (*Ananas comosus*)

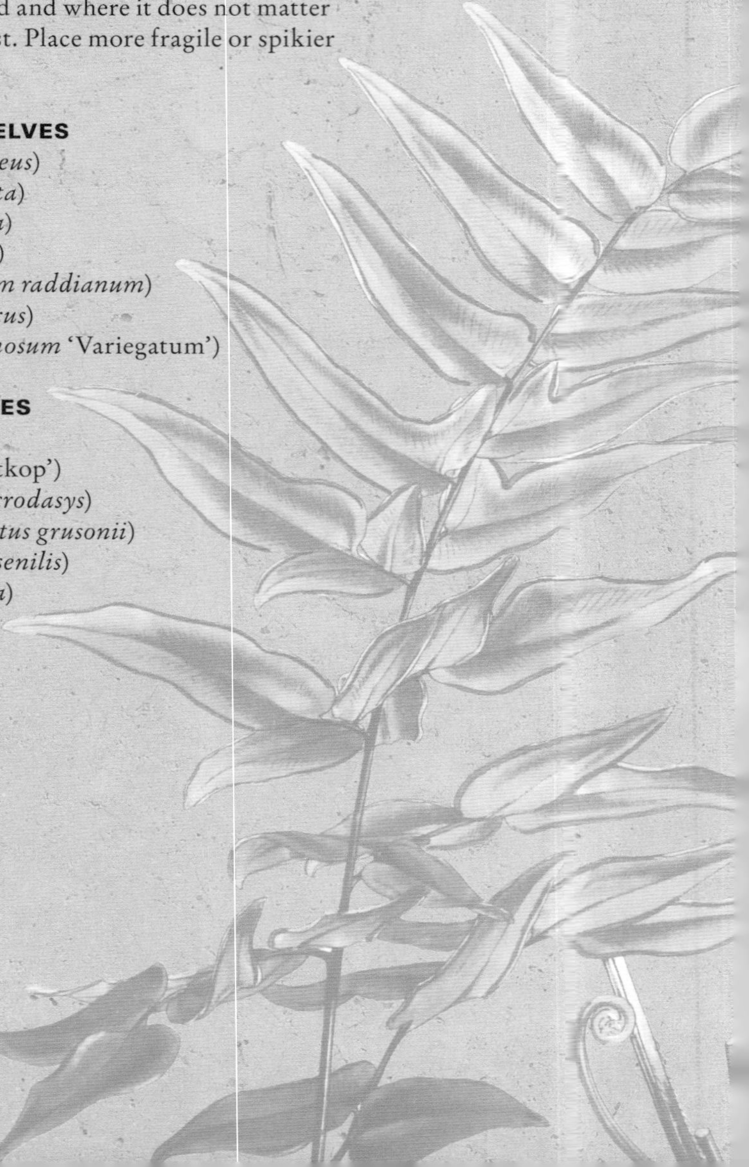

1 The soft, feathery foliage of asparagus fern cries out to be touched.
2 Soothe burnt skin with the cooling gel of Barbados aloe. Cut a leaf at the base and slice into segments, then hold each upside down to release the gel.
3 The succulent, spiky-edged leaves of Barbados aloe are easily bruised and broken, so place this plant at the top of the display ladder.
4 Fill each step with plants or else stagger them up the ladder.

Amazonian elephant's ear

Alocasia x *amazonica* aka African mask, jewel alocasia

An exotic showstopper with huge, arrow-shaped leaves that are glossy, wavy and heavily marked along the veins and margins in white. These are real head-turners, but they are trickier to grow than many other house plants, demanding constant warmth, humidity and moisture.

—

WHERE TO GROW

Amazonian elephant's ear prefers indirect light but not shade – if in too dark a spot, plants can become elongated and floppy. A warm, light kitchen or steamy bathroom would be ideal. Keep out of draughts and away from radiators.

HOW TO GROW

Mist leaves every day to keep humidity levels up. The rhizome will rot if kept too wet so water lightly, using rain- or filtered water, every couple of days from spring to autumn. In winter, allow the compost to dry out completely between watering. Feed with a balanced liquid fertilizer every few weeks from spring to autumn. Repot every couple of years.

GROWING TIP

Wipe the foliage regularly to keep it dust-free and glossy (see also Natural air fresheners, page 124).

Family Araceae

Temperature
18–25°C/65–77°F

Light Bright but indirect light

Water Keep the compost moist in growing season

Height and spread
1.2x1m/4x3ft

CONFUSING NAME
Although *Alocasia* comes from the forests of Asia and Australia, *A.* x *amazonica* is a horticultural hybrid named after the nursery where it was developed – it is not from the Amazon!

Alocasia longiloba

Barbados aloe

Aloe vera aka Curaçao aloe

Barbados aloes are tough plants, making them brilliantly undemanding and easy to look after. Their rosettes of spiky, fleshy leaves provide architectural interest and, if growing well, striking flower spikes of yellow blooms are borne in summer. Their plump leaves contain a translucent gel that soothes sore, irritated or burnt skin; to access it, just snip off a leaf (see page 41). Partridge breast aloe (*A. variegata*) is lovely, too, with blotchy, stripy leaves.

—

WHERE TO GROW
The fleshy leaves are used to arid conditions so a warm, sunny, even south-facing windowsill above a radiator suits Barbados aloe well.

HOW TO GROW
Grow in a free-draining, 50:50 mix of potting compost and grit, perlite or sand. Water well and then allow the compost to almost dry out before watering again. Over winter, reduce watering to just once a month. Feed a couple of times in the growing season.

GROWING TIP
Move plants outside in summer. The fresh air will give them a boost.

AIR FRESHENER
Barbados aloe is one of the top plants for purifying the air in your home, absorbing benzene and formaldehyde (see also Natural air fresheners, page 124).

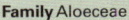

Family Aloeceae

Temperature 8–27˚C/46–80˚F

Light Bright, sunny, indirect light

Water Sparingly

Height and spread 60x60cm/24x24in

43

Pineapple

Ananas comosus

This knock-out feature plant has dense rosettes of prickly edged, strappy leaves. After yellow and purple flowers it will produce your very own pineapple fruit from the centre, although this is purely ornamental and inedible with a bitter taste. *Ananas comosus* var. *variegatus* has yellow-and-green-striped leaves.

—

Family Bromeliacea
Temperature 16–29˚C/61–84˚F
Light Sunny
Water Moist
Height and spread 60x90cm/24x36in

WHERE TO GROW

The floor or a tabletop in a warm, bright room would make a better home than a shelf, which might cramp the arching leaves.

HOW TO GROW

Grow in a 50:50 mix of orchid compost and multipurpose compost. Plants need high humidity to fruit so mist every day or grow on a tray of wet pebbles. Water well in spring and summer and then reduce to keeping the compost just moist in winter. Give a liquid feed every two weeks in the growing season. Baby offsets at the base can be removed and grown on into new plants (see page 31).

GROWING TIP

If your plant is getting too large, restrict its size by growing it in a heavy stone pot 15cm/6in in diameter.

PROPAGATION USES

Although the pineapple growing from the middle is not edible, a new plant can be propagated from it – simply remove it, cut off the leafy top and trim off the bottom leaves, then pot on the stem. Water sparingly until new growth appears and then keep moist.

Tail flower

Anthurium andraeanum aka flamingo flower, lace leaf, oil cloth

Tail flowers are popular, stylish plants with dark, shiny leaves and dramatic flowers that can last year-round. This species has a bright red spathe with a white spadix covered in tiny, yellow flowers, but there are also stylish white, pink and darker burgundy forms such as *A.* Pink Champion and *A.* Black Queen. All are easy-going and quite simple to grow.

Family Araceae

Temperature
16–24°C/61–75°F

Light Bright, indirect light

Water Keep moist but not soggy

Height and spread
45x30cm/18x12in

WHERE TO GROW
Tail flower requires warmth, high humidity and protection from direct sunlight so a bright bathroom is perfect.

HOW TO GROW
Water lightly every day if growing in a warm room and mist plants daily to keep the humidity levels high. Feed with a liquid fertilizer every other week in the growing season. When repotting, ensure the top of the root ball sits just above the surface of the compost; then cover with a layer of mulch so that it does not dry out.

GROWING TIP
Make sure your pot has good holes in the base so that water can drain away freely.

FLOWER PARTS
The 'bloom' of a tailflower is in fact a waxy, leaf-like spathe with a long flower spike, or spadix, in the centre.

Asparagus fern

Asparagus setaceus aka feathery fern

Despite its common name, asparagus fern is not a true fern but a member of the lily family and close relative of the edible asparagus. This elegant plant has delicate, lacy foliage and a bushy habit that starts to climb with the help of spines on the stem as the plant matures. Foxtail fern (*A. densiflorus*) bears dense, feathery, bottlebrush-like 'fronds' and is lovely in a hanging basket or tall planter or on shelving.

WHERE TO GROW

A light kitchen is a good choice because direct light scorches the leaves, but too little light makes the foliage fade to a jaundiced yellow. Plants can be trained up supports or left to scramble downwards from a shelf.

HOW TO GROW

Feed every month in spring and summer. Reduce watering in winter, allowing the top of the compost to dry out before watering again. When plants are root-bound, repot into a new pot just one size larger.

GROWING TIP

Keep plants looking their best by misting occasionally, particularly in winter when the central heating is on.

Family Asparagaceæ

Temperature
10–25°C/50–77°F

Light Semi-shade or dappled sunlight

Water Keep moist in growing season

Height and spread
3x3m/10x10ft

JOB DIVISION
The tiny, needle-like leaves are actually flattened stems or cladodes, and these perform photosynthesis rather than the true leaves, which are the minuscule scales between the cladodes and the stem.

Cast-iron plant

Aspidistra elatior aka bar room plant

Tough as old boots, this stately plant is aptly named and has long been a household favourite for good reason – it thrives in dry shade. It bears strappy, dark green leaves and looks good when grown in groups. Look out for cultivars with interesting variegation in the form of striping or splashes, such as *A. elatior* 'Asahi'.

—

WHERE TO GROW

These are forgiving plants that can cope with both warm or cold temperatures so grow them where more fussy plants will fail. Variegated plants need a lighter spot than plain-leaved species, if markings are not to fade.

HOW TO GROW

Cast-iron plant tolerates pretty much anything but overwatering, so make sure its pot and compost are free-draining and do not leave it sitting in water. Feed monthly in spring and summer.

GROWING TIP

Wipe leaves weekly with a damp cloth, to keep them dust-free (see Natural air fresheners, page 124).

Family Asparagaceae

Temperature 5–20°C/41–68°F

Light Shade, semi-shade

Water Wait for the top 2cm/¾in of compost to dry out between watering

Height and spread 60x60cm/24x24in

GLORY DAYS REVIVED A Victorian favourite, cast-iron plant fell out of favour but is back in fashion thanks to its easy-going nature.

Bird's nest fern

Asplenium nidus aka shield fern

Handsome rosettes of shiny, strappy fronds form an upright shuttlecock with new baby fronds curled up in the base. The fronds of *A. nidus* 'Crispy Wave' are attractively crinkled and ruffled along the edges.

—

WHERE TO GROW

A north- or east-facing window is ideal, provided that this easy-to-grow plant is out of draughts and bright light. Its need for humidity makes the bathroom the perfect choice.

HOW TO GROW

Mist plants every day, particularly in winter, or place each on a saucer of wet pebbles. Feed every other week from spring to early autumn. Wipe the fronds regularly to keep them shiny and free from dust (see Natural air fresheners, page 124). Repot in spring every couple of years.

GROWING TIP

Water the edge of the compost rather than over the fronds, which can cause the rosette to rot.

Family Aspleniaceae

Temperature 12–25°C/54–77°F

Light Semi-shade, dappled light

Water Moist

Height and spread 60x40cm/24x16in

FROND FUNCTION
Unlike in other ferns, the fronds are not divided but entire and are excellent at helping to purify the air.

Ponytail palm

Beaucarnea recurvata aka elephant's foot

Ponytail palm is a truly star plant with its distinctive bulbous stem, or caudex, and shock of narrow leaves. At home in the arid deserts of Mexico, the swollen caudex is an adaptation for storing water during drought, so this easy-to-grow plant will forgive a long holiday or missed watering.

WHERE TO GROW

Give the ponytail palm a bright, sunny spot.

HOW TO GROW

Grow in a free-draining compost with an equal quantity of perlite or grit mixed in. Water plants once a week in the growing season. Allow plants to dry out completely over winter. Being slow-growing – it can live for hundreds of years in the wild – ponytail palm does not need repotting very often.

GROWING TIP

This plant likes a snug home in a pot only slightly bigger than the width of its stem.

Family Asparagaceae

Temperature
15–25°C/59–77°F

Light Bright, sunny, direct light

Water Allow to dry out between watering

Height and spread
2x1m/7x3ft

COMMON NAME ANOMALY
The ponytail palm is actually closely related to the yucca (see page 140).

Making a decorative screen

Windowsills are a predictable place to grow house plants, but why not use these plants as a screen to provide privacy or to mask an unsightly view? Such a green barrier is particularly useful in bathrooms and bedrooms, or any room that is overlooked, and it will instill a feeling of calm.

Plants that have an upright habit but will not block out too much light are key to a successful decorative screen, so opt for plants such as snake plant, cast-iron plant, fern arum and asparagus fern – choosing your plants according to the light levels at your window.

Traditional window boxes work well – just be sure to block off any drainage holes with silica gel to stop water leaking out, or else line your sill with plants in individual pots. If using a trough as a cover pot, drop your plants into it, staggering them so they make a dense screen.

1 When planting into a trough, add a layer of gravel or grit to the base to help with drainage and to improve air flow. Then half fill with compost. Remove each plant (here, *Sansevieria bacularis* 'Mikado') from its pot and set so it is at the correct depth.
2 Insert the remaining plants, then fill and top off with compost and firm down. Water the plants in well.

Painted-leaf begonia

Begonia species

Very different beasts to their brash bedding plant cousins these are beautiful foliage plants with bold spots and swirls, stripes and splashes. There are hundreds of forms to choose from, many hybrids of *B. rex*, but there are also cane-stemmed types, which are taller and have larger flowers.

—

WHERE TO GROW
These are plants that need to be seen close up, so grow them in a prominent spot on a table or sideboard that is away from draughts and the drying heat of a radiator, particularly in winter.

HOW TO GROW
Raise humidity around plants by placing each on a saucer of pebbles and water rather than misting the leaves, which are susceptible to powdery mildew. Feed every couple of weeks in the growing season with a nitrogen-rich fertilizer, switching to a high-potash one when buds appear on forms grown for their flowers. Allow the compost to dry out between watering in winter.

GROWING TIP
Cane-stemmed types may need staking to stop plants flopping over.

Family Begoniaceae

Temperature
15–22°C/59–72°F

Light Bright shade, indirect light

Water Moist but not wet in growing season

Height and spread
Up to 90x50cm/36x2◼in

COMMON ANCESTOR
Begonia semperflorens (now called *B. cucullata*), illustrated here, is the ancestor of the common bedding begonia, first described in 1829.

OTHER NOTABLE CULTIVARS

- *B.* 'Black Fang' is a rhizomatous type with almost black leaves, each with a bright green star in the centre, as well as pretty, pink flowers. Leaves will revert to green if light levels are too low.
- *B.* 'Escargot' is one of the most popular rex begonias with snail-shell-patterned, swirling leaves in green and silver.
- *B. maculata* 'Wightii' produces long stems, large, spotty leaves and trailing clusters of white flowers. This cane-type polka dot begonia is perfect for bringing structure to a display.
- *B.* 'Red Tempest' has mesmerizing, twisting, silver leaves painted with dark green veins and red blushes at the centres.

Old man cactus

Cephalocereus senilis aka monkey cactus, old man's head

This woolly cactus with its white, old man's beard is a favourite among house plant growers, thanks to its striking, columnar looks. The hairs insulate it against frost and extreme heat, and may also conceal formidable spines.

—

WHERE TO GROW

Give this a sunny windowsill – the brighter the spot the more the hairs (which protect it from the heat) will grow, but shield it from the intense heat of the sun through the glass in summer.

HOW TO GROW

Use a coarse, free-draining compost mix (see Compost mixes, page 22). Water from the bottom to protect old man cactus from rotting, and in winter water only every few weeks. Repot plants every other year, in spring.

GROWING TIP

Too little light causes the stem to elongate and grow thin so keep it in a bright spot, especially in winter.

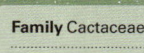

Family Cactaceae

Temperature 10–32°C/50–90°F

Light Bright, sunny

Water Allow to dry out completely before watering

Height and spread 30x10cm/ 12x4in

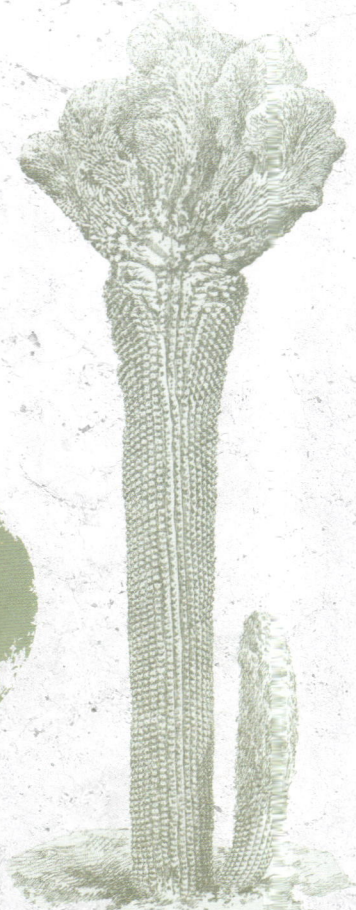

BALDING PATTERN
As the plant ages and its skin thickens and increases its ability to withstand temperature extremes, old man cactus will start to lose its hairs.

String of hearts

Ceropegia linearis subsp. *woodii* aka hearts on a string, rosary plant, sweetheart vine

This is a lovely-looking, trailing vine with delicate, cotton-like stems and heart-shaped leaves. It is surprisingly tough, easy to grow and very drought-tolerant thanks to the root tubers it develops to store water as it matures. If happy, string of hearts will flower in late summer, producing little, pink, tubular blooms.

Family Apocynaceae

Temperature
8–24°C/46–75°F

Light Bright, sunny

Water Let top of compost dry out before watering in growing season

Height and spread
10x90cm/4x36in

WHERE TO GROW
Give this plant pride of place on a shelf or in a basket, where it can tumble down and show off. It is happy in a humid spot so a bathroom would suit it well. Although string of hearts prefers a bright spot, it copes with shade but its lacy leaves may lose some of their pretty colouring. It also tolerates temperature change.

HOW TO GROW
Grow in a free-draining mix of 50:50 potting compost and perlite. Feed every couple of weeks in spring and summer. In winter, water only when the compost is almost completely dry. Repot when the plant is root-bound.

GROWING TIP
Snip off stems and pot up (see Propagation by stem cuttings, page 29); such cuttings root easily.

DUE REWARD
Discovered hanging from rocks at 500m/1,640ft in South Africa by the curator of Durban Botanic Garden John Medley Wood in 1881, string of hearts was sent to RBG Kew in 1894 and was named after him.

Parlour palm

Chamaedorea elegans aka dwarf mountain palm

A favourite in the parlours of the Victorians and popular ever since thanks to its easy-going nature and tolerance of low light levels, this is one of the easiest feature plants you can grow. It bears feathery fronds and develops a compact, slender habit. If it is happy, tiny, yellow sprays of flowers will appear once it is mature.

—

WHERE TO GROW
This slow-growing palm is perfect for a shady spot in any room – too harsh a spot will turn the leaves yellow. It likes humidity so keep it away from the drying heat of radiators, particularly in winter.

HOW TO GROW
Mist the leaves regularly, particularly in winter when the air will be dry. Feed monthly in the growing season. In winter, reduce watering so that the compost is almost dry. Cut out any brown fronds at their bases.

GROWING TIP
Wash dust from the fronds by standing the plant under a tepid shower or outside in summer rain during the warmer months.

Family Arecaceae

Temperature
10–27°C/50–80°F

Light Semi-shade

Water Allow the top of the compost to dry out between watering

Height and spread
1.2x0.6m/4x2ft

HEALTH BENEFITS
The parlour palm is on NASA's top 50 plants for cleaning the air because of the way its lush fronds aid this process (see also Natural air fresheners, page 124).

Spider plant

Chlorophytum comosum 'Variegatum'

A seventies' favourite but still a timeless classic, spider plant is one of the easiest house plants going. Its striped, arching leaves and endearing, dangling offsets give it its distinctive look.

—

WHERE TO GROW

Being native to tropical and southern Africa where it grows on the forest floor, spider plant is tolerant of both light and shade. However, you should avoid direct sunlight, which will scorch the leaves, while at the same time appreciating that a shadier home will produce fewer plantlets.

HOW TO GROW

Thanks to its tuberous root, the odd period of drought in the growing season will do no harm. Water sparingly in winter, allowing the compost to dry out completely before watering again. Feed plants every 2–3 weeks in spring and summer. Repot every couple of years when it becomes pot-bound.

GROWING TIP

In the wild, baby plantlets root wherever they touch soil. Grow on such plantlets by planting them into individual pots of compost (see page 33).

Family Asparagaceae	
Temperature 7–25°C/45–76°F	
Light Indirect light, dappled shade	
Water Moist	
Height and spread 50x30cm/20x12in	

CHOICE SETTINGS
Spider plant is perfect for a hanging basket or when grown cascading over a shelf.

Natal lily

Clivia miniata

Natal lilies are beautiful, clump-forming plants. Their strappy, deep green leaves form a showy, layered bulbous stem as they grow. Jubilant, tall spikes of trumpet flowers in orange or red are borne from mid-spring to late summer and are followed by large berries containing fleshy seeds. Look for butter-yellow-flowered *C. miniata* var. *citrina*. Natal lily exudes an irritating sap so wear gloves when handling the plants.

WHERE TO GROW

Through spring and summer grow it in a warm room, but during winter transfer it to a cooler spot, at just 10°C/50°F, to allow the plant to rest and to promote flowering. Keep away from the dry heat of a radiator.

HOW TO GROW

Plant so that the neck of the bulbous root is just above the surface of the compost. Give a low-strength general feed every month from spring to autumn. Stop watering in winter and move to a cooler room until flower buds are spotted; then place back in the warmth, *c.*16°C/61°F. Cut flower spikes off at the base as they fade.

GROWING TIP

Natal lily grows best when snug around the roots so do not repot unless it is literally bursting from its pot.

Family Amaryllidaceae

Temperature 10–23°C/50–73°F

Light Dappled light

Water Allow to dry out between watering

Height and spread 50x30cm/20x12in

ROYAL CONNECTION
In 1828 Kew botanist John Lindley named the genus *Clivia* in honour of a governess of Queen Victoria – the Duchess of Northumberland, Charlotte Percy (née Clive) – who was the first to grow and bring *Clivia* to flower.

Jade plant

Crassula ovata aka money tree, friendship tree

One of the easiest and low-maintenance house plants, jade plant is extremely tolerant of neglect and almost indestructible thanks to its thick, fleshy, oval leaves. When given plenty of light, tiny, star-shaped, pink or white flowers will appear in late winter and spring. The silver jade *Crassula arborescens* is similar, but has silvery leaves.

WHERE TO GROW

A warm, sunny, south- or west-facing windowsill suits jade plant well and promotes the pretty, red edges to the leaves.

HOW TO GROW

Grow in a free-draining mix of equal quantities of potting compost and perlite. Water sparingly in the growing season and hardly at all in winter, just often enough to stop the leaves shrivelling and drying out. Feed once in spring and again in summer.

GROWING TIP

Jade plant grows according to the size of its pot, but, whichever size you choose, make it a sturdy one as plants can be top-heavy.

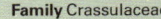

Family Crassulaceae

Temperature
15–25°C/59–77°F

Light Bright, sunny, dappled light

Water Allow to dry out between watering

Height and spread
2.5x1.5m/8x5ft

GOOD GIFT
Jade plant is simple to share by propagating from stem or leaf cuttings (see pages 28–9). Let cuttings dry out and the wound callus over before potting on into moist compost.

Sago palm

Cycas revoluta aka cycad

An eye-catching plant with its rough-textured trunk and sturdy, upright (surprisingly sharp) fronds, this is not a true palm but part of an ancient group of plants called gymnosperms that date back to the dinosaurs, 65½ million years ago.

—

WHERE TO GROW
Sago palm has a beautiful symmetry that deserves pride of place in a living room. Just keep it away from draughts and radiators or other heat sources. Avoid direct sun, which will cause scorching.

HOW TO GROW
This plant is very tolerant of drought and low temperatures. Water only the compost or from below (see page 23), as any water on the crown will cause it to rot. Feed once a month in spring and summer, and mist the fronds in summer. Leave plants almost dry in winter.

GROWING TIP
When new fronds appear, do not move a sago palm. As they unfurl, the fronds arrange themselves to receive maximum light, and if you move the plant they will twist.

Family Cycadaceae

Temperature
5–24°C/41–75°F

Light Bright

Water Allow the top of the compost to dry out before watering

Height and spread
1.5x1.5m/5x5ft

CULINARY CHALLENGE
In their native home cycads are used to make sago, which involves a lengthy process to carefully wash out toxins – all parts of the palm being poisonous to humans and animals. Always keep these plants away from pets.

Dumb cane

Dieffenbachia seguine aka leopard lily

These lush, impressive plants produce huge, oval leaves with splashes and splotches of dark green, lime-green and cream.

—

WHERE TO GROW

Happy by an east- or west-facing window out of bright direct light, this is a statement plant for a main living area. Dumb cane dislikes draughts and the drying heat from radiators.

HOW TO GROW

Mist plants or stand each on a tray of pebbles. Feed monthly in spring and summer. Keep the compost on the drier side of moist in winter.

GROWING TIP

Wear gloves when repotting, to protect against the toxic sap in the leaves and stem. Keep pets away.

Family Araceae	
Temperature 16–23°C/61–73°F	
Light Filtered sun or semi-shade	
Water Moist	
Height and spread 1.5x1.5m/5x5ft	

BE ALERT

The common name dumb cane comes from the toxic sap in the leaves and stems, which causes swelling and blistering in the mouth if eaten and can be severe enough to prevent speaking and swallowing.

A shallow bowl of succulents

Drought-loving succulents with their plump, fleshy leaves provide us with a whole host of dramatic shapes, textures and colours. They are also undemanding, easy plants to grow that love a warm, bright spot, making them ideal for growing together in an attractive planter in the heat of a sunny windowsill. Use a mix of your favourite succulents but select a large focal plant such as a jade plant or black aeonium, to add height and draw the eye.

Add a good layer of gravel to the base of a container with plenty of drainage holes, to help improve air flow and drainage and prevent your plants from sitting in water. Use a free-draining cactus compost or make your own (see page 22).

Plant your focal plant first and then add the rest, leaving room between plants for them to grow. Use your fingers to firm the compost around each plant. Pretty pebbles, shells and stones will help to personalize your display. Move your succulents to a bright spot near a window and water only when the compost feels completely dry.

—

GOOD SUCCULENTS FOR DISPLAY
Barbados aloe (*Aloe vera*)
Black aeonium (*Aeonium* 'Zwartkop')
Crassula ovata 'Hobbit'
Jade plant (*Crassula ovata*)
Mexican gem (*Echeveria elegans*) and others
Moonstone (*Pachyphytum oviferum*)
String of pearls (*Kleinia rowleyana*)

1   Assemble your succulents
    (here, *Crassula ovata* 'Hobbit'
    and *Echeveria*), compost, grit,
    a suitable container and a
    decorative gravel or horticultural
    grit for topdressing that
    contrasts well with the container.
2   Make a free-draining mix to suit
    your succulents (see page 22).
3   Remove each plant from its pot
    and gently tease out its roots,
    to encourage growth. Place it in
    the compost and firm well.
4   Topdress the compost and
    between the plants. This will
    hold moisture in the soil.
5   Water the plants in.

Venus fly trap

Dionaea muscipula

Insects are lured with nectar to this very popular carnivorous plant with its hinged, snapping leaf traps. These are triggered by an insect or spider touching the tiny hairs scattered across its leaf surface. The teeth in the traps are wide enough to allow lucky, smaller insects to escape – they are not worth the effort involved in digesting them!

Family Droraceae	
Temperature 9–27°C/48–80°F	
Light Sunny	
Water Moist	
Height and spread 10x20cm/4x8in	

WHERE TO GROW

A south-facing windowsill away from radiators is ideal. Ensure your plant gets food by opening the window, to allow insects in, or leave it outside for a few days at a time in summer.

HOW TO GROW

Grow Venus fly trap in a nutrient-poor potting mix (see Carnivorous plants, page 22) and keep it almost saturated in spring and summer, by placing its pot on a saucer of soft rain-, filtered or distilled water. Remove this in winter when the plant is dormant, but keep the compost still moist, always watering from below (see page 23). Plants do not need feeding. Repot every year as Venus fly trap hates being cramped (see also Carnivorous vase, pages 68–9).

GROWING TIP

White flowers appear in spring, but nip these out so that the plant can concentrate its energies in the leaves.

NOT A TOY
Resist the temptation to keep coaxing Venus fly trap to snap shut its jaws. The effort involved will kill it.

Dragon tree
Dracaena marginata aka Madagascar dragon tree

This is an exotic-looking, upright plant with grassy, red-edged leaves sprouting from multiple woody stems, while *Dracaena fragrans* bears fountains of broad, glossy leaves. *D.* 'Janet Craig' is tolerant of shadier spots than these two species.

—

WHERE TO GROW
Dragon tree is ideal for a bright, north- or east-facing room, but keep it close to the window as it suffers in very gloomy shade.

HOW TO GROW
Mist or group plants together to improve moisture levels around them. Feed monthly in the growing season. Being surprisingly drought-tolerant, dragon tree hates sitting in soggy soil so allow the top of the compost to start drying out before watering in winter. Prune back if a plant gets too tall, using loppers or a pruning saw if the trunk is thick and tough. New shoots will sprout in a couple of weeks.

GROWING TIP
Keep the toxic leaves away from pets, particularly cats which seem to find them particularly appetising.

Family Asparagaceae

Temperature
15–24°C/59–75°F

Light Indirect light/
semi-shade

Water Moist in growing
season

Height and spread
1.5x1m/5x3ft

EASY CARE
Dragon tree is at home in the semi-arid desert areas of Africa and is low-maintenance and easy to grow, tolerant of both erratic watering and a shady spot.

Cape sundew

Drosera capensis

These colourful, glistening plants catch their food with sticky traps – rosettes of long, slim leaves with red tentacles covered in globules of sticky mucilage (they look like water, or dew, hence the name). These catch insects and the leaves then wrap around the prey, trapping it until it is absorbed by the plant.

Family Droseraceae

Temperature
7–29°C/45–84°F

Light Sun, filtered sun

Water Moist

Height and spread
15x20cm/6x8in

WHERE TO GROW
Position on a bright, sunny windowsill. Cape sundew is more forgiving than other carnivorous plants, tolerating the odd, short-lived fluctuation in temperature.

HOW TO GROW
Grow in a nutrient-poor potting mix (see Carnivorous plants, page 22). Always water Cape sundew from below (see page 23) and use soft rainwater, filtered or distilled water rather than tap. Keep plants constantly moist and humid by growing them on a saucer of water in spring and summer. Remove this in winter when the plant is dormant but still keep the compost moist. Plants do not need feeding (see also Carnivorous vase, pages 68–9).

GROWING TIP
In late spring or early summer, pretty, pink flower spikes are borne, but each lasts just a day. Nip these out to stop plants self-sowing into nearby plant pots.

MEAGRE FARE
Cape sundew is good at catching midges, mosquitoes and small houseflies, although it can survive on just two or three insects a month.

Golden cane palm

Dypsis lutescens aka Areca palm, butterfly palm

A graceful, tufted palm with arching, feathery fronds, this is a popular plant that is cultivated extensively in gardens in warm climates.

—

WHERE TO GROW

These palms make wonderful focal points in a hallway or living area. A bright spot will enhance the yellow in their upright stems and intensify the lush, green fronds.

HOW TO GROW

Golden cane palm dislikes sitting with soggy roots, so tip excess water away. It prefers a humid life so mist every day or two. Feed twice a month in spring and summer. Repot in spring when plants are pot-bound.

GROWING TIP

Be prepared to water your plant often as it transpires heavily, losing 1 litre/1¾ pints of water in just twenty-four hours.

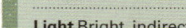

Family Arecaceae

Temperature 13–24°C/55–75°F

Light Bright, indirect light

Water Allow to dry out between watering

Height and spread 3x1m/10x3ft

STAR BILLING
Golden cane palm is rated by NASA as one of the best plants for removing indoor air pollution (see also Natural air fresheners, page 124).

Carnivorous vase

Carnivorous plants are an intriguing group that are much easier
to look after than you might think. Most of them simply require
boggy, slightly humid conditions and a sunny spot. They can
be grown individually in a pot and saucer, but as most have
similar cultural needs they can also be planted together to make
a fascinating feature. Collections look good when grown in low
troughs or shallow planters, but are also happy in large glass
vessels such as this round, fishbowl-style vase.

Carnivorous plants are fussy about soil and demand moisture-
retentive, ericaceous soil so use a specialist carnivorous compost
mix or make your own peat-free potting mix (see page 22).
Such plants need to be kept constantly moist from spring to
autumn, so line and topdress your container with moss to help
to retain water and give plants the boggy conditions they love.
Carnivorous plants are also very sensitive to water type. The
minerals and salts in tap water, particularly hard water, will build
up and eventually kill them so always collect and use rainwater
to water them with. Carnivorous plants do not require feeding.

—

CARNIVOROUS PLANTS
FOR A VASE
Cape sundew (*Drosera capensis*)
North American pitcher plant (*Sarracenia flava*)
Venus fly trap (*Dionaea muscipula*)

1. Line the vase base and sides with moss.
2. Add a generous layer of carnivorous compost.
3. Remove each plant (here, North American pitcher plant) from its container.
4. Plant in the compost. Fill in around the plants with more compost if necessary and firm down, to remove any air pockets.
5. Topdress with a layer of moss.
6. Water in the plants. To do this in a round vase, carefully aim the water at the side of the vase so that it goes directly into the compost rather than splashing over the plants.

Moulded-wax succulent

Echeveria agavoides aka wax agave

This species is just one of a huge group of rosette-forming succulents that come in countless shades of green, silver and red with leaves that can be plump, flat, fuzzy, crinkled or smooth. All produce brilliantly coloured flowers on long stems. Moulded-wax succulent has thick, deep green leaves, which turn bronze at the tips in very bright light.

—

WHERE TO GROW

Grow on a bright, sunny windowsill as too little light will make the rosette start to elongate.

HOW TO GROW

Plant in an open, free-draining compost mix (see Cacti and succulents, page 22). Water regularly in spring and summer, but give none when dormant, when plants should be moved to a cooler spot (6–10°C/43–50°F) to promote flowering the following year. Feed just a couple of times in the growing season. When plants are root-bound, repot in spring.

GROWING TIP

Baby plantlets at the base of the plant can be removed and grown as new plants (see page 31) or be left to form a larger group of plants. Moulded wax succulent can also be increased by leaf cuttings (see page 28).

Family Crassulaceae

Temperature 6–30°C/43–86°F

Light Bright sun or filtered sun

Water Allow the top of the compost to dry out between watering

Height and spread 10x30cm/4x12in

OTHER NOTABLE SPECIES AND CULTIVARS

- *E.* 'Doris Taylor' (woolly rose) is beautifully hairy, with fuzzy, green leaves and reddish tips.
- *E. elegans* bears beautiful, blue-green leaves with very pointy tips and flowers that are pink on the outside and orange within.
- *E.* 'Perle von Nürnberg' has a lovely, purple sheen to its fleshy leaves.

ON THE RECORD
Many *Echeveria* come from Mexico and were named after a Mexican naturalist and botanical artist, Atanasio Echeverria y Godoy, who compiled an inventory of its flora and fauna in the eighteenth century.

Golden barrel cactus

Echinocactus grusonii aka golden ball, mother-in-law's cushion

Eye-catching golden barrel cactus is rounded with green flesh, a fluffy, yellow crown and distinctive ribs of very sharp, golden spines. As it ages, it become more oblong, and the spiny ribs are more dramatically pronounced. Mature plants bear large, sunny yellow flowers.

—

WHERE TO GROW
Place on a sunny windowsill and open the window occasionally in summer so plants can enjoy the fresh air. Avoid humid rooms such as a bathroom and kitchen.

HOW TO GROW
Grow in a free-draining potting mix (see Cacti and succulents, page 22). Water regularly in spring and summer. Give plants minimal water in winter. Feed a couple of times in the growing season. Repot when plants are root-bound, but wear very thick gloves or wrap plants in layers of paper to protect your hands. Plants grow quickly when young but then slow right down and so need repotting less.

GROWING TIP
The green flesh can mark if conditions are too humid so move the plant to a drier spot if this occurs.

Family Cactaceae	
Temperature 12–32°C/54–90°F	
Light Sunny, bright light	
Water Allow to dry out between watering	
Height and spread Up to 50x50cm/20x20in	

SPECIAL PLACES
Endemic to Mexico, plants can live up to thirty years but are rare in the wild, occurring in only a couple of areas following the creation of the Zimapán Dam in the state of Hidalgo.

Hedgehog cactus

Echinopsis aurea aka sea-urchin cactus, Easter lily cactus

The globular hedgehog cactus is covered in dense, long, curly spines and, in summer, stunning, bright butter-yellow flowers on long, tubular stems are borne in the evenings.

—

WHERE TO GROW

Position on a warm, sunny windowsill in the growing season but keep out of direct sun. To promote flowering, hedgehog cactus requires a period of winter cold so move it to a cool, bright window with a minimum temperature of 5°C/41°F.

HOW TO GROW

Although hedgehog cactus likes a free-draining potting mix (see Cacti and succulents, page 22), it does need more water than typical cacti. Water regularly in spring and summer. In winter, it requires little, if any water. Repot plants every two years.

GROWING TIP

Do not saturate plants. They have soft, fibrous roots that will rot if kept too wet.

Family Cactaceae	
Temperature 5–32°C/41–90°F	
Light Bright, indirect light	
Water Allow to dry out between watering	
Height and spread 10x20cm/4x8in	

EXTENDED OPENING
Flowers usually appear once plants reach two to three years old. Often, many buds develop on one plant and open in flushes over several days.

Fishbone cactus

Epiphyllum anguliger aka zigzag cactus, ric rac cactus

These are wonderfully weird-looking plants – mounds of long, flattened, wiggly leaves dangle outwards, making them perfect for a spot centre stage in your house.

—

WHERE TO GROW

The hanging leaves tend to make plants top-heavy so grow them in hanging baskets or in heavy stone pots on a shelf, to prevent them from tumbling over.

HOW TO GROW

Plant in a free-draining cactus compost mix (see page 22). Mist plants daily or stand each on a tray of wet pebbles. Water regularly, in spring and summer, and feed monthly in the growing season. In autumn and winter, keep the compost just moist.

GROWING TIP

Fishbone cactus prefers a cooler, shadier spot during winter. Move the plant back to a minimum of 16°C/61°F in spring.

Family Cactaceae

Temperature
10–25°C/50–77°F

Light Bright, indirect light, semi-shade

Water Allow to dry out between watering

Height and spread
60x60cm/24x24in

NOCTURNAL TREAT
After four or five years, beautiful, fragrant flowers bloom at night during autumn. These are followed by edible, kiwi-like fruits.

73

Desert islands

All cacti and succulents have strong individual textures, from
fleshy leaves to spiky stems, and a great way to show off their
many different shapes and sizes is to group them together. To
reinforce the relationship between them and to draw the eye to
the individual plants rather than distract from them, select pots
that are exactly the same or very similar. Here, I have chosen
simple, white pots as a contrast to the plants and to highlight the
variations in their textures and form, and have then drawn them
all together by standing them within a large stone platter. Each
pot has also been topdressed with crushed oyster shell, which
sets off the plants and helps to keep moisture away from their
stems. Place the display in a sunny spot.

Water your desert plants only when their compost is dry,
taking care not to splash the plants. Leave them to dry out
completely between mid-autumn and early spring.

—

PLANTS FOR A DESERT DISPLAY

African spear (*Sansevieria cylindrica*)
Bunny-ears cactus (*Opuntia microdasys*)
Golden barrel cactus (*Echinocactus grusonii*)
Old man cactus (Cephalocereus senilis)
Pincushion cactus (*Mammillaria* species)
Sansevieria kirkii 'Silver Blue'
Zebra cactus (*Haworthia fasciata*)

1 When repotting, wrap newspaper around spiky cacti (here, *Pilosocereus pachycladus*), to avoid getting prickled.

2 Use a small, soft paintbrush to carefully clean away excess compost or grit from plants (here, *Mammillaria elongata*).

3 The distinct, white stripes of *Haworthia fasciata* 'Alba' match the pots beautifully.

4 *Sansevieria kirkii* 'Silver Blue' has a low, spreading habit and is perfect for the front of a display.

5 The trick to harmonizing your display is to grow the cacti in matching containers.

Devil's ivy

Epipremnum aureum aka golden pothos, silver vine, scindapsus, Ceylon creeper

The perfect plant for nervous growers, this tough, easy plant will still reward the odd forgotten watering with its trailing stems and large, marbled, heart-shaped leaves.
—

WHERE TO GROW
Lovely in a hanging basket or cascading from a shelf, these quick growers can equally be trained to grow up a moss pole. In a group these rampant plants are a great way to screen areas, too. Keep away from draughts and the drying heat of a radiator. Also position plants away from pets, as all parts of devil's ivy are toxic.

HOW TO GROW
Grow in multipurpose potting compost. Water year-round, keeping the compost moist except in winter, when it should be just moist. Take care not to overwater, which causes rot. Feed plants monthly in the growing season. Repot every couple of years.

GROWING TIP
New plants are easily propagated in spring from stem cuttings (see pages 28–9).

Family Araceae

Temperature
18–24°C/65–75°F

Light Bright, indirect light

Water Moist

Height and spread
2x2m/7x7ft

CLEANER AIR
Devil's ivy is excellent at removing toxins and chemicals such as formaldehyde, xylene and benzene from the air (see also Natural air fresheners, page 124).

Candelabra plant

Euphorbia lactea 'Cristata' aka cactus euphorbia

Candelabra plant is actually a combination of two plants (*Euphorbia lactea* and *E. neriifolia*) grafted together to create this brain-like habit. Such striking, sculptural plants – more cactus-like than succulent in appearance – have modified stems (as opposed to the modified leaves of cacti) that have developed into thorns.
—

WHERE TO GROW
A south-facing windowsill suits this weird-looking plant, but protect it from midday rays in the height of summer.

HOW TO GROW
Grow in a coarse, free-draining cactus compost mix (see page 22) so that water can drain away freely; never leave plants sitting in water. In winter, keep the compost almost dry. Feed monthly during active growth.

GROWING TIP
The lower graft occasionally suckers; this can be removed (see page 31) or be left, depending on your preference.

Family Euphorbiaceae

Temperature
10–30°C/50–86°F

Light Bright/indirect light

Water Allow compost to dry out between watering in the growing season

Height and spread
Up to 90x60cm/36x24in

SKIN IRRITANT
All *Euphorbia* contain white, milky sap, which is painfully irritating to the skin, so handle plants with care and wear gloves – you will also avoid their nasty thorns. Keep children and pets away.

OTHER NOTABLE SPECIES

- *E.tirucalli* (cactus pencil) is like a miniature tree, with slender, smooth, green branches. Tiny leaves sprout on new stems but are soon shed.
- *E. trigona* (African milk tree) has spiny, upright, cactus-like stems with small, green leaves sprouting attractively from the tips.

Fiddle-leaf fig

Ficus lyrata aka banjo fig

This statuesque plant with large, leathery, slightly crumpled leaves is top of many house plant growers' wish list despite it being a somewhat temperamental house guest. Look for comparatively compact *Ficus lyrata* 'Bambino', which reaches just 1m/39in tall.

—

WHERE TO GROW

Position in front of an east- or west-facing window away from cold draughts and radiators – anywhere, in fact, where temperature swings are common.

HOW TO GROW

Plant in a 3:1 mix of soil-based potting compost and perlite. Keep the humidity up in summer by misting the leaves every few days and preferably grow plants in groups. Figs are sensitive to both over- and underwatering so let the compost dry out between watering and then water really well. Feed monthly in the growing season. Reduce watering in winter, so that the compost is just moist. Repot every few years.

GROWING TIP

Fiddle-leaf fig is often sold as a single-stem plant, but it can be pinched out to encourage branching and to achieve an attractive, tree-like shape.

Family Moraceae	
Temperature 15–24°C/59–75°F	
Light Bright, indirect light	
Water Allow to dry out between watering	
Height and spread 1.8x1.2m/6x4ft	

UNGRATEFUL
In the wild these are banjan figs, which start life as an epiphyte on another tree, then send roots down to the ground and eventually strangle the host tree.

Mosaic plant

Fittonia albivenis Verschaffeltii Group aka nerve plant, silver net plant

These striking, little ground-cover plants have dark green leaves with each and every vein picked out in white, pink or red. They can be a little tricky and need their growing conditions just right, but give them the exact warmth and moisture they require and they will fully reward you.

WHERE TO GROW
Grow the mosaic plant in a steamy bathroom or by the kettle in the kitchen. It is also a great terrarium plant (see Miniature rainforest, page 118).

HOW TO GROW
Mosaic plants thrive in high humidity so mist them every morning or place each on a tray of pebbles. If too dry, plants wilt quickly and spectacularly but should recover just as speedily when they are watered well. Feed monthly in the growing season. Pinch out the small, summer flowers so that energy is concentrated on the leaves.

GROWING TIP
Plants root well from stem cuttings (see pages 28–9) so are easy to propagate into new plants for friends or yourself.

Family Acanthaceae

Temperature
17–26°C/63–79°F

Light Filtered sun

Water Moist, year-round

Height and spread
15x20cm/6x8in

DUAL PURPOSE
The marked veining is more than good looks – it helps the plants trap as much light as possible in the limited levels found deep within the rainforest.

Fairy elephants' feet

Frithia pulchra aka baby toes, elephant's baby toe

Fairy elephants' feet is tough, tiny and brilliantly easy to grow. It is a stemless plant producing clusters of erect, modified leaves with 'windows' at their tips, to protect them from extreme harsh light and heat.

—

WHERE TO GROW

Position by a sunny window, opening it at times in spring and summer so that the plant can enjoy the fresh air.

HOW TO GROW

Fairy elephants' feet needs a very coarse, open compost (see Cacti and succulents, page 22). It will rot if too wet so water sparingly in the growing season and hardly at all in winter. If plants get too dry they draw themselves into the ground or compost, to protect themselves; if this happens, increase the watering. Feed every few weeks in the growing season.

GROWING TIP

Plants must be happy, with plump leaves, if they are to produce their showy, bright pink, white-centred, daisy-like flowers in winter.

Family Aizoaceae

Temperature 18–26°C/65–79°F

Light Bright, sunny

Water Dry

Height and spread 10x20cm/4x8in

LASTING GIFT
Frithia was first established as a genus in 1925 by a Kew botanist, N.E. Brown. He named it after Frank Frith, the gardener at Park Station in Johannesburg, who took the plant to Brown when he visited London.

Cape jasmine

Gardenia jasminoides aka common gardenia

An evergreen garden shrub in warmer climes, this is a lovely house plant for a living space, where its gorgeously heady scent will fill the room. It is beautiful, too, with large, waxy, white flowers shining out from glossy, green leaves.

—

WHERE TO GROW

These plants like even temperatures so position them away from cold draughts and heat sources. As the light levels drop in winter, move to a sunny windowsill.

HOW TO GROW

Grow in ericaceous compost, and water with rain- or filtered water – tap water contains too much calcium for this acid-lover. It likes high humidity so regularly mist the plant (avoiding the flowers) or grow on a saucer or tray of pebbles topped up with water. In winter, allow the top of the compost to dry out before watering.

GROWING TIP

To ensure flowering, keep plants at a steady 21–4°C/70–5°F during the day and at 15–18°C/59–65°F during the night.

Family Rubiaceae

Temperature
15–24°C/59–75°F

Light Bright, indirect light or filtered sun

Water Moist in growing season

Height and spread
60x60cm/24x24in

ARTISTIC ATTRACTION
The *Gardenia* genus has been cultivated in China for more than 1,000 years – it can be seen, in both wild and double forms, in paintings dating back to AD 960.

Peacock plant

Goeppertia makoyana aka calathea, cathedral windows

Just one of a large group of stunning, leafy evergreens, peacock plant has striking blotches and purple undersides to its leaves. Others include *G. zebrina*, which produces broad leaves with pinky-white zebra stripes, and *G. insignis*, which has wavy-edged, slender leaves with snake-like markings in lime-green and dark green.

—

WHERE TO GROW
Find it a warm spot in a room with high humidity.

HOW TO GROW
Remove excess water so the compost is moist but not soggy. Peacock plant loves humidity so mist plants daily or sit on a tray of pebbles and water. Feed every couple of weeks in spring and summer. For a thriving plant, repot every year.

GROWING TIP
If the leaves start to roll up, it is a sign that the plant is drying out, so water well to keep the compost moist.

Family Marantaceae

Temperature
16–24°C/61–75°F

Light Indirect light/shade

Water Keep the compost moist year-round

Height and spread
60x50cm/24x20in

VITAL COLOUR
The purple undersides to the leaves is an environmental adaptation that helps plants catch the dim light within the forest.

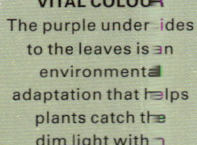

Goeppertia zebrina

Scarlet star

Guzmania lingulata aka tufted air plant, tongue-shaped guzmania

The dazzling flower spike of this epiphyte is its main attraction, with vibrant scarlet and orange bracts shooting from the centre of the rosette of glossy, green leaves. Small, white and yellow flowers can be seen within. There are many hybrids and cultivars with yellow, orange and purple bracts.

WHERE TO GROW
Grow on a table or shelf, rather than on a windowsill – the beautiful flowers and striking leaves make this a perfect centrepiece. Plants can also be tied to bark or a piece of wood and bound with moss.

HOW TO GROW
Grow it in a 50:50 mix of orchid compost and multipurpose compost. Keep the central well topped up with rain-, filtered or distilled water so that it is always at least 2cm/¾in full. Mist the whole plant – leaves, bracts, flowers and aerial roots – daily. Feed once a month with a diluted liquid feed watered into the well; tip this out after a few days and replace with rainwater.

GROWING TIP
Scarlet star is happiest when its roots are snug, and this helps promote flowering.

Family Bromeliaceae	
Temperature 15–27°C/59–80°F	
Light Bright, indirect light	
Water Water the inner well and let the compost dry out between watering	
Height and spread 45x45cm/18x18in	

BORN ANEW
Like other bromeliads, scarlet star dies after flowering, but not before producing offsets at the base. These can be grown on into new plants.

83

Hanging gardens

Suspending plants in the air is a great way to make the most of every bit of space in a room; they draw the eye upwards, too, so the room feels bigger. Suitable containers for hanging come in all sorts of designs and materials, from ceramic and metal to the glass planters shown here. Or you can buy or make your own macramé-style hangers, to slip pots into. Remember that plants are heavier after watering, so make sure that hanging materials are strong enough to hold them.

All hanging planters are best used as cover pots rather than final containers, to avoid plants sitting in water. This also makes watering easier and prevents accidental splashes of water over the floor and furniture. Before watering, remove each plant from its hanging planter; having watered it, allow it to drain, then replace in the planter.

PLANTS FOR HANGING GARDENS

Creeping fig (*Ficus pumila*)
Devil's ivy (*Epipremnum aureum*)
Donkey's tail (*Sedum morganianum*)
Heart leaf (*Philodendron scandens*)
Mistletoe cactus (*Rhipsalis baccifera*)
Silver-inch plant (*Tradescantia zebrina*) and others
Spider plant (*Chlorophytum comosum* 'Variegatum')
Staghorn fern (*Platycerium bifurcatum*)
String of hearts (*Ceropegia linearis* subsp. *woodii*)
String of pearls (*Kleinia rowleyana*)
Wax flower (*Hoya carnosa*)

1 Mist plants such as this mistletoe cactus regularly, to keep humidity levels high.
2 Secure plants from hooks in the ceiling, rafters or shelves, or suspend them from a curtain pole or coat rack.
3 *Tradescantia* 'Green Hill' makes a striking feature plant with its pretty, white flowers and leaves that are purple underneath.
4 When hung in front of a window, plants (here, spider plant, mistletoe cactus and *Tradescantia* 'Green Hill') will create a living curtain of greenery.

Zebra cactus

Haworthia fasciata aka pearl plant, star window plant

A tidy, little plant with a rosette of spiky, triangular leaves, zebra cactus resembles an aloe (see page 43) but has distinctive markings, including those with raised, white stripes or pink bumps. It is an easy house plant to grow, tolerating lower light levels than other succulents.

—

WHERE TO GROW

Set on an east- or west-facing windowsill. In displays, zebra cactus contrasts beautifully with other cactus and rounder-leaved succulents such as moulded-wax succulent (see page 70).

HOW TO GROW

Grow in a coarse, open, free-draining compost (see page 22). Water plants well in spring and summer; in winter, water only occasionally. Feed once a month in spring and summer.

GROWING TIP

Offsets – 'pups' – can be easily removed; leave them to dry out for a couple of days and then plant up as new, individual plants (see page 31).

Family Asphodelaceæ

Temperature 12–26°C/54–79°F

Light Bright light or filtered sun

Water Allow to dry out between watering

Height and spread 15x15cm/6x6in

OTHER NOTABLE SPECIES

- *H. attenuata* 'Striata' is very similar to zebra cactus and difficult to tell apart.
- *H. limifolia* has a flatter, more open habit and very fine, white stripes.

RED FOR DANGER
When exposed to too much sun or deprived of water, the zebra cactus will change colour to red or purple.

Bellmore sentry palm

Howea forsteriana aka kentia palm, thatch palm

Bring a touch of the tropics to your living space with this elegant, architectural palm. Endemic to Lord Howe Island in Australia, it will eventually reach a height of 3m/10ft, but slowly – this plant is a long-term investment. Fortunately, it is a toughie and very easy to look after.

—

WHERE TO GROW
Although plants tolerate a lot, they will always look their best when given moist, humid conditions and indirect light. They will thrive in front of a north- or east-facing window.

HOW TO GROW
Mist regularly or give them a shower in tepid water or outside in summer rain. Feed every two weeks from spring to autumn. Allow the compost to dry out between watering in winter. These palms dislike disturbance so repot them carefully only when plants are particularly root-bound, and only topdress larger plants.

GROWING TIP
To create a bushier look, Bellmore sentry palm is often sold with more than one plant in a container.

Family Arecaceae	
Temperature 13–24°C/55–75°F	
Light Indirect light or semi-shade	
Water Moist in growing season	
Height and spread 3x2m/10x7ft	

PROTECTIVE VIGIL
Bellmore sentry palms graced most houses during the Victorian era, and Queen Victoria loved them so much she instructed that they were to be placed around her coffin when she lay in state.

Wax flower

Hoya carnosa aka wax vine, porcelain flower, Hindu rope plant

These gorgeous, tropical creepers have waxy leaves and sweetly scented, pale pink flowers that look strangely artificial. They appear in summer and can drip with sticky nectar in the mornings. *Hoya lanceolata* subsp. *bella* has a more compact habit and is perfect for a small room.

—

WHERE TO GROW

Plant this fast grower in a basket or loop it around wire. It is actually tolerant of deep shade and drought, but to flower it requires brighter light and moister compost.

HOW TO GROW

Grow in an open potting mix that comprises an equal quantity of multipurpose compost and perlite. Mist plants regularly but not when in flower, or grow them on a tray of pebbles and water. Feed every two weeks in the growing season. In winter, allow the top of the compost to dry out between watering. Plants flower better when a little snug, so keep them slightly root-bound.

GROWING TIP

Once flowers fade, they produce further blooms so do not snip out the knobbly spurs.

Family Asclepiadaceae

Temperature 16–24°C/61–75°F

Light Bright, indirect light

Water Moist in growing season

Height and spread 4x4m/13x13ft

NOT JUST A PRETTY FACE
Wax flower is excellent at removing pollutants from the air (see also Natural air fresheners, page 124).

Polka dot plant

Hypoestes phyllostachya aka flamingo plant, freckle face, baby's tears

These jaunty little plants are brightly spotted with pink, red, light green or white speckles on their heart-shaped leaves – there are many cultivars (and some can look a little gaudy). They are undemanding but relatively short-lived and get tattier with age so eventually need replacing.

Family Acanthaceae

Temperature 18–27°C/65–80°F

Light Bright, indirect light

Water Allow top to dry out between watering

Height and spread 30x30cm/12x12in

WHERE TO GROW
Above the kitchen sink or in a bathroom are ideal spots, but place them back from a window. However, if set in too dark a spot, the leaves can revert to solid green. These are great plants for growing in a terrarium (see Miniature rainforest, page 118).

HOW TO GROW
Polka dot plant needs the top of its compost to dry out between waterings in the growing season. Mist plants every few days, group with others or stand on a tray of pebbles and water, to keep humidity levels up. Feed every two weeks from spring to autumn. In winter, keep compost just moist. After a couple of years plants will flower in summer and then slip into a dormant phase – just reduce watering until new shoots appear.

GROWING TIP
Pinch out the stem tips to encourage a bushier, neater plant.

WATCH OUT
Plants seed freely outside, and garden escapees in warmer countries have made polka dot plant an invasive weed.

Jasmine

Jasminum polyanthum aka scented Chinese jasmine, pink jasmine vine

The star-shaped blooms have an intoxicating scent that is particularly heady at night, and the lobed, deep green leaves make this the prefect package. For a little more variety, *J. polyanthum* 'Variegata' has creamy yellow-edged leaves.
—

WHERE TO GROW
Keep away from draughts and radiators, particularly in winter. Too warm a room will prevent the plant from flowering. These vigorous growers will twine themselves around hoops or up supports.

HOW TO GROW
Water plants regularly in spring and summer, particularly when plants are in bud and flower. After that, allow them to dry out a little. Feed every two weeks, from spring to autumn. Plants prefer to be tightly packed into their pots, so repot them only when young; topdress larger plants with fresh compost.

GROWING TIP
To ensure plants flower again, prune jasmine hard after flowering, reducing the main stems and side shoots to 2–3cm/¾–1¼in.

Family Oleaceae

Temperature
10–24°C/50–75°F

Light Filtered sun

Water Moist in growing season

Height and spread
3x3m/10x10ft

FLORAL TREAT
The flowers of this heavenly scented, twining climber appear copiously in late winter and spring.

Flower-dust plant

Kalanchoe pumila aka dwarf kalanchoe, quicksilver

These are lovely, little, easy-care plants with dusty grey leaves that are appealingly toothed with pinking-shear edges. In winter and spring, plants bear clusters of dusky pink and purple flowers at the ends of sprawling stems.
—

WHERE TO GROW

Needs a bright spot in a south-facing window in an airy room. Its pendent habit makes it perfect for a hanging basket or to trail over a shelf or windowsill.

HOW TO GROW

Grow in an open, free-draining compost mix (see Cacti and succulents, page 22). To protect the foliage, water from below (see page 23). In autumn and winter, the compost can be kept almost dry. Feed plants monthly from spring to late summer.

GROWING TIP

Deadhead faded blooms, then give the plant a rest, reducing watering until new growth begins.

USEFUL NAME
The *pumila* in the botanical name means 'low-growing' or 'small' – referring to this plant's diminutive stature.

OTHER NOTABLE SPECIES

- *K. blossfeldiana* (flaming Katy) is neat, little plant with fleshy, green leaves and long-lasting, slightly garish flowers in red, pink, white and yellow in spring and summer.
- *K. tomentosa* (panda plant) is far more subtle, with dusky grey, fuzzy leaves that are tipped with brown and are velvety to the touch. Plants can reach 60cm/24in and make an understated centrepiece.

Family Crassulaceae	
Temperature 12–27°C/54–80°F	
Light Full sun or bright, indirect light	
Water Let the top of the compost dry out before watering in the growing season	
Height and spread 30x30cm/12x12in	

String of pearls

Kleinia rowleyana aka string of beads

The cascading strings of pea-like beads, or 'pearls', make this plant top of many house plant collectors' lists. Although it looks fragile, it is brilliantly tough and a great plant for beginners, as it is more than capable of coping with neglect. In spring, small, white, daisy flowers may appear.

—

WHERE TO GROW

String of pearls is perfect for a table or desk or hanging in a south-facing window. Give the plant cooler conditions in winter, no less than 10°C/50°F, to encourage flowering. Plants are toxic to humans and animals, so keep them well out of the way of pets and little fingers.

HOW TO GROW

Grow in a gritty cactus compost mix (see Cacti and succulents, page 22). Feed once a month in spring and summer. Make sure the plant never sits in water. In winter, water very sparingly; if the beads start to shrivel, the compost is too dry. Trim plants if needed in spring (and grow the prunings on as stem cuttings, see pages 28–9). Repot every two or three years, taking care not to break the stems by holding them carefully in your hand.

GROWING TIP

Whenever a stem touches soil, or compost, it takes root so this is a very easy plant to propagate.

Family Asteraceae

Temperature
10–25°C/50–77°F

Light Sun or bright indirect light

Water Let the top of the compost dry out before watering in the growing season

Height and spread
5x90cm2x36in

THE NATURAL WAY
We may grow it in hanging pots and baskets, but in its native environment plants creep across the ground rooting as they go, to form dense mats of green beads.

Living stones

Lithops aka pebble plants

These amazing, low-lying plants are composed of two swollen leaves with a slit in between, which produces new leaves and flowers. Some varieties have speckled or patterned markings, others bear spots, while many are plain glaucous green. In late summer and autumn, they produce white or yellow, daisy-like flowers. They are easy to look after, making them ideal for the forgetful waterer, and they are also great for arousing children's interest.

WHERE TO GROW
Give them a hot, south-facing window year-round. Warmth is particularly important in winter, when the light levels drop but plants are still growing.

HOW TO GROW
Plant in a sharply draining cactus compost mix (see page 22). In winter, spring and summer, water plants as soon as the leaves start to shrivel. In autumn, increase watering so that the leaves stay constantly firm. Too much water can cause plants to burst, while plants will shrink and can disappear below the surface of the compost if conditions get too dry. Feed plants just once, in autumn.

GROWING TIP
Slow-growing living stones prefers to be cultivated in an individual pot rather than in a combined display. It requires potting on only very rarely.

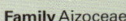

Family Aizoceae	
Temperature 18–26°C/65–79°F	
Light Sunny	
Water Water sparingly	
Height and spread 2.5x1cm/1x½in	

CAMOUFLAGE
In order to avoid being eaten, these plants have evolved to resemble the pebbles and stones that litter their native South African desert floor.

Pincushion cactus

Mammillaria species aka powder puff cactus, nipple cactus

Pincushion cactus is a popular house plant that is generally easy to look after. It is small, often rounded or columnar, and covered in spines. In summer, it rewards growers with a 'crown' of brightly coloured flowers.

—

WHERE TO GROW
These plants are ideal for a bright windowsill. In summer, move them out of direct, scorching sun.

HOW TO GROW
Plant in a sharply draining cactus compost mix (see page 22). Feed once a month in the growing season. In winter, when plants are dormant, water just a couple of times. Repot plants carefully, wearing gloves, every couple of years in spring. Plants are easy to propagate by offsets (see page 31).

GROWING TIP
During the dormant season, move plants to a cool, bright, dry room away from a radiator and other heat sources.

Family Cactaceae

Temperature
7–30°C/45–86°F

Light Sunny or bright, filtered light

Water Let the top of the compost dry out before watering in the growing season

Height and spread
15x30cm/6x12in

FLORAL CROWN
Pincushion cactus has distinctive tubercles – tiny bumps that cover the surface of the plant and from which spines and flowers grow.

NOTABLE SPECIES

- *M. plumosa* (feather cactus) has a mass of dense, long, white spines that cover the flesh of the plant. Small, creamy white flowers are produced in summer.
- *M. spinosissima* are cylindrical cacti that can reach 30cm/12in and are covered in long, auburn spines. They bears pink flowers in summer.
- *M. zeilmanniana* (rose pincushion cactus) is one of the easiest to grow; it has clustered stems and bright pink-purple flowers.

Prayer plant

Maranta leuconeura var. *kerchoveana* aka rabbit tracks, rabbit's foot

These striking plants have leaves that appear to be hand-painted. The undersides are red, but the upper leaf surfaces have dark and light green blotches and veins picked out in red across each leaf. Prayer plant is trickier to grow than some house plants but is less demanding than its other cousins in the family.

WHERE TO GROW

Position away from cold draughts and the drying heat of radiators or other sources.

HOW TO GROW

Mist leaves every few days or place on a tray of pebbles and water to raise humidity around the plant. Growing it in a group with other plants also helps. Feed every two weeks in spring and summer. Allow the compost to dry out slightly between watering, in winter.

GROWING TIP

Young plants will thrive in a humid terrarium or bottle garden (see Miniature rainforest, page 118).

Family Marantaceae

Temperature
15–24°C/59–75°F

Light Bright, indirect light

Water Moist in the growing season

Height and spread
60x60cm/24x24in

FOLDING FOLIAGE
The common name prayer plant derives from the way the leaves, which are flat and open during the day, endearingly fold together at night, like hands in prayer.

Maranta leuconeura var. *massangeana*

Windowsill propagation

Many house plants can be propagated as leaf cuttings rooted in compost (see page 28) or in water. Using the latter technique they make a lovely temporary display while rooting. Even plants that cannot be increased in this way but have beautiful leaves can be chosen to create a vibrant and interesting water garden. Display them in plain or coloured glasses, small bottles or pretty vases that are in proportion to the leaf cuttings and position them on a windowsill or shelf, or group them as a centrepiece for your table.

—

PLANTS THAT MAKE GOOD CUT LEAVES
Asparagus fern (*Asparagus setaceus*)
Chinese evergreen (*Aglaonema commutatum*) – also roots in water
Devil's root (*Epipremnum aureum*) – also roots in water
Dwarf umbrella tree (*Schefflera arboricola*)
Fern arum (*Zamioculcas zamiifolia*)
Foxtail fern (*Asparagus densiflorus*)
Goeppertia 'Whitestar'
Peace lily (*Spathiphyllum wallisii*)
Peacock plant (*Goeppertia makoyana*)
Prayer plant (*Maranta leuconeura* var. *kerchoveana*)
Rose grape (*Medinilla magnifica*)
Spider plant (*Chlorophytum comosum* 'Variegatum') – also roots in water
String of hearts (*Philodendron xanadu*) – also roots in water

1 Remove a leaf (here, devil's root) from the base or stem of the plant and cut it to size, at a 45-degree angle, so that it sits comfortably in its glass. Such an angled cut maximizes the amount of water absorbed.

2 Half-fill a glass or vase with water and place the leaf cutting with others in a group (here, fern arum, peace lily, spider plant and Amazonian elephant's ear).

3 Change the water every few days, to keep it fresh, and replace spent leaves when needed.

4 Once roots have formed in the water, you can plant rooted stems straight into compost in a new pot or else leave them as they are in the water.

Rose grape
Medinilla magnifica aka pink lantern, Philippines orchid

When this truly exceptional plant blooms it stops you in your tracks. The large, heavily veined, deep green leaves are wonderful on their own, but the hanging, lipstick-pink, papery bracts and flowers are something else. It is called rose grape after the pink flower buds that hang from its bracts, like bunches of tiny grapes.

—

WHERE TO GROW
Grow this epiphyte in a tall pot or on a shelf so that it can dangle over the edge. An east- or west-facing window is ideal; just make sure it still gets plenty of light in winter.

HOW TO GROW
Plant in orchid compost, and water from below (see page 23). Raise the humidity by misting the leaves every other day or by growing on a tray of pebbles and water. Feed every two weeks from spring to summer. In winter, water just enough to stop the compost drying out completely; resume more regular watering when flowers stems are visible. Deadhead the blooms as they fade.

GROWING TIP
Encourage this plant to reach its fully mature size by repotting it every two to three years. It should grow to a magnificent 1m/39in tall and wide.

Family Melastomataceae

Temperature
17–25°C/63–77°F

Light Bright, indirect light

Water Allow the compost to dry out between watering, in the growing season

Height and spread
1x1m/39x39in

REGAL NOTE
In the 1990s, King Baudouin of Belgium was so devoted to rose grape that he grew it in his conservatories and they were depicted on the Belgian 10,000 franc note.

Swiss cheese plant

Monstera deliciosa aka fruit salad plant, ceriman

With its beautifully holey, heart-shaped leaves and climbing habit, Swiss cheese plant has long been a house plant favourite, although this seventies classic did fall out of favour for a few years. It is back with a vengeance now and very easy to grow, as long as you have plenty of space for it.

—

WHERE TO GROW
It is the perfect plant to transform a negative space or dull corner – provided it is not too gloomy nor too shady as new leaves will not then have their distinctive holes. Swiss cheese plant is often sold clinging to a mossy pole but it can also be left to sprawl or climb over your own support.

HOW TO GROW
Water as soon as the compost feels dry, but in winter allow it to dry out a little. Mist the leaves (and the moss pole if it is grown up one) every couple of days or grow on a tray of pebbles and water. Feed monthly in the growing season. Prune in spring, to keep Swiss cheese plant in check.

GROWING TIP
The more content the plant, the larger the leaves will grow.

Family Araceae

Temperature
18–27°C/65–80°F

Light Bright, indirect light/semi-shade

Water Moist in the growing season

Height and spread
8x2.5m/26x8ft

EVOLUTION
Native to the tropical rainforests of Panama and Mexico, the leaves of Swiss cheese plant have become ribbon-like to allow light and water through to the plant roots below.

Blushing bromeliad

Neoregelia carolinae f. *tricolor*

One of the most dazzling house plants, this sprawling bromeliad has a flat, open rosette of yellow-striped leaves that blush bright red at the centre when it is about to flower. Small, violet flowers appear deep inside the well in summer, but it is the bright bracts that are the main attraction.

—

WHERE TO GROW
Position by an east- or west-facing window, giving the plant centre stage on a dining or coffee table. Too much sun scorches the leaves while too little causes its colours to fade.

HOW TO GROW
Grow in a 50:50 mix of orchid compost and multipurpose compost. Keep the central well topped up with rain-, filtered or distilled water, so that it is always at least 2cm/¾in full. Water when the top of the compost feels dry. Mist the leaves every few days. Feed plants once a month by spraying the leaves with a diluted liquid feed.

GROWING TIP
Like other bromeliads, this one dies after flowering, but not before producing offsets at the base of the rosette. These can be grown on into new plants (see page 31).

Family	Bromeliaceae
Temperature	18–27°C/65–80°F
Light	Bright, indirect light
Water	Moist
Height and spread	30x60cm/12x24in

FLORAL ALERT
The bright colours at the centre of the rosette are a sign to nearby pollinators that the plant is about to flower.

Monkey cups

Nepenthes sanguinea aka tropical pitcher plant

Carnivorous monkey cups is a scrambling, climbing plant that catches insects and other small creatures in its deep, hanging pitchers, which fill with water and then drown their prey. A vigorous grower with pretty, burgundy pitchers to 30cm/12in long, it is more forgiving than others in its family when it comes to cultural conditions and care.

Family Nepenthaceæ

Temperature
13–24°C/55–75°F

Light Filtered sun

Water Moist

Height and spread
30x45cm/12x18in

WHERE TO GROW
Ideal for a hanging basket in a bright, humid room or placed on a shelf above the bath or the kettle in the kitchen.

HOW TO GROW
Grow in an open, low-nutrient compost mix (see Carnivorous plants, page 22). Mist every day or stand on a tray of pebbles and water, to keep humidity levels up. Unlike other carnivorous plants, monkey cups can be fed in summer with a foliar feed every couple of weeks (see also Carnivorous vase, page 68).

GROWING TIP
Keep out of direct light; these plants are at home in shady rainforests and too bright light will scorch their leaves.

GIANT RELATIVE
Closely related to monkey cups is *N. rajah,* which grows on the slopes of Mount Kinabalu and is the largest carnivorous plant in the world. Its giant pitchers measure as much as 40x20cm/16x8in.

Boston fern

Nephrolepis exaltata aka sword fern, ladder fern, fishbone fern

A popular and easy-to-grow plant, Boston fern produces a beautiful fountain of abundant green, cascading fronds.

WHERE TO GROW

Boston fern is perfect for the bathroom or a busy kitchen. If growing in a drier room, mist daily or place on a saucer of pebbles and water. With its ruffled, arching habit, it is magnificent in a hanging basket or flowing over a shelf, and if allowed it can become a large statement plant.

HOW TO GROW

Mist plants daily (see above), and feed them monthly from spring to autumn. Reduce watering in winter, so that the compost starts to dry out. Plants keep growing the more room you give them so repot every spring.

GROWING TIP

Regularly turn plants grown on shelves, as they have a habit of going bald at the back. Any fronds that die back or are scorched can be cut off at the base.

Family Nephrolepidaceae

Temperature
12–24°C/54–75°F

Light Bright, indirect light/ semi-shade

Water Moist in growing season

Height and spread
60x90cm/24x36in

LONG-LASTING
N. exaltata 'Bostoniensis' is the classic Boston fern prevalent on plant stands in Victorian parlours and still available today.

Bunny-ears cactus

Opuntia microdasys aka polka dot cactus, angel's wings

Endemic to the Mexican desert, this striking architectural cactus has distinctive, flattened stem pads that are dotted with clusters of tiny prickles. These are not spines but glochids – hair-like, barbed prickles that are grouped together in areoles across the pad. Once mature, plants bear large, deep yellow flowers in spring and early summer on the tips of the pads.

—

WHERE TO GROW
A south-, west- or east-facing window is ideal for the growing season; it prefers a cool room in winter. Position it somewhere it will not be knocked into or brushed against – the tiny hairs come off and imbed themselves into hands or arms very easily (and painfully).

HOW TO GROW
Grow in a coarse, open, free-draining compost mix (see page 22). In spring and summer, water plants weekly. When the plant is dormant it needs very little; just water once or twice – a little more if it is near a radiator or fire. Feed plants every couple of months, from spring to autumn.

GROWING TIP
The barbed glochids come off much more easily than the true spines on other cacti so this plant is not one to be grown around children or pets.

Family Cactaceae

Temperature
10–30°C/50–86°F

Light Bright/indirect light

Water Let the compost dry out before watering

Height and spread
60x45cm/24x18in

AIDING SURVIVAL
The flat pads are modified stems or cladodes that have evolved to help the plant cope with drought.

False shamrock

Oxalis triangularis aka love plant

These endearing plants have shamrock-like, purple leaves held at the end of delicate, straggly stems. Although dainty clusters of pale pink flowers last for several weeks in spring and summer, false shamrock's most endearing feature is that its leaves respond to light by opening during the day and then gently closing together at night. It also has a fibrous bulbous root system, which makes it the perfect house guest for forgetful waterers.

—

WHERE TO GROW

Give false shamrock a front-row seat on a table or windowsill and then move somewhere less obvious when dormant in winter.

HOW TO GROW

Plant in a free-draining potting compost with equal parts of perlite mixed in. Feed monthly in spring and summer. In winter, the bulb is dormant, the leaves die back and false shamrock needs no water. Begin watering again after a couple of months; new growth will soon appear.

GROWING TIP

Plant new bulbs in autumn, ensuring each is 5cm/2in below the surface of the compost.

Family Oxalidaceae

Temperature
15–21°C/59–70°F

Light Bright, indirect light or semi-shade

Water Let the compost dry out between watering in the growing season

Height and spread
30x30cm/12x12in

FOOD ALERT
Although false shamrock has a tangy lemony flavour and makes a colourful addition to salads or pesto, it should be eaten in moderation because of the oxalic acid it contains.

Picture perfect

Many house plants that are grown for their spectacular foliage are as eye-catching as a work of art, and if you snip off a leaf and insert it in a frame it can become one. When hung in a window, plants with thinner leaves will allow the light to shine through, illuminating their colours; or select intricately shaped foliage and lean your frame against a wall, to create striking silhouettes.

Use specialist frames that have two pieces of glass, or simply buy two cheap frames and use the glass from both instead of the backing board in just one frame. You can flatten thicker leaves first between the pages of a heavy book protected by baking paper.

As leaves fade, replace them with fresh ones or allow them to take on sepia hues for a different look.

—

PLANTS FOR PICTURE FRAMES
Amazonian elephant's ear (*Alocasia* x *amazonica*)
Bellmore sentry palm (*Howea forsteriana*)
Bird's nest fern (*Asplenium nidus*)
Boston fern (*Nephrolepis exaltata*)
Button fern (*Pellaea rotundifolia*)
Cretan brake fern (*Pteris cretica*)
Delta maidenhair fern (*Adiantum raddianum*)
False shamrock (*Oxalis triangularis*)
Prayer plant (*Maranta leuconeura* var. *kerchoveana*)
String of hearts (*Philodendron xanadu*)
Swiss cheese plant (*Monstera deliciosa*)

1 Lay your chosen leaves (here, Boston fern, bird's nest fern and delta maidenhair fern) carefully on the bottom pane of glass and then gently lower the top pane on to them. Line up the panes and slide them into the frame

2 Press down firmly, then seal the frame and hang it in a window so that the leaf textures are lit up as sunlight shines through them.

Moonstone

Pachyphytum oviferum aka sugar almond plant

Moonstone has plump, fleshy leaves that are the shape of pebbles (hence the common name) or sugared almonds nestled on the surface of the compost. They are a pretty, greeny blue with a dusty bloom. In late winter, long stems burst from the centre of the leaf whorl bearing striking, pink flowers surrounded by fleshy, greeny grey sepals.

WHERE TO GROW

Position on or near a sunny windowsill, especially in winter when light levels are naturally low.

HOW TO GROW

Grow in a free-draining cactus compost mix (see Cacti and succulents page 22) so that water can flow away from the roots. Water plants from below (see page 23) so that water does not mark the leaves. These plants are in active growth in winter so step up the watering during winter months.

GROWING TIP

Repot after flowering only when plants are root-bound.

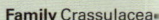

Family	Crassulacea
Temperature	10–27°C/50–80°F
Light	Bright light or sun
Water	Let the compost dry out before watering
Height and spread	10x30cm/4x12in

DERIVATION
Pachyphytum oviferum literally means 'thick plant bearing eggs'.

Pachyphytum longifolium

Geranium

Pelargonium species

They are easy to look after, forgiving of the odd dry spell. Popular types include those with scented foliage, zonal pelargoniums with their dark ring markings on the leaves and regal pelargoniums, which have clusters of large flowers.

—

WHERE TO GROW

An east- or west-facing windowsill is ideal, to avoid scorching midday sun in summer.

HOW TO GROW

Plants like good drainage so add a handful of grit or perlite to the compost when planting. Water plants well, making sure you do not get water on the leaves or flowers. In winter, water sparingly, keeping the compost almost dry. Feed with a general fertilizer every couple of weeks in spring and then with a high-potash one in summer, to promote flowering. Repot in spring.

GROWING TIP

Geraniums are naturally bushy and should be cut back in early spring, before growth begins, to encourage branching.

Family Geraniaceae

Temperature
7–25°C/45–77°F

Light Sun or bright, indirect light

Water Let the top of the compost dry out before watering in the growing season

Height and spread
40x25cm/16x10in

LONG-LIVED FLOWERS
Nearly all *Pelargonium* species are indigenous to semi-desert parts southern Africa. Many will flower in winter as well as summer, if grown indoors.

Button fern

Pellaea rotundifolia aka New Zealand cliff brake

This charming, little fern has tufted, arching fronds made up of small, button-shaped leaves. It has a light, delicate air and adds a lovely symmetry to group displays and plantings. Endemic to the forests and scrub of New Zealand, it does not need the high humidity and constant moisture that most ferns need and is, therefore, easy to care for.

WHERE TO GROW

Although good in a bathroom, button fern is ideal for an open terrarium (see Miniature rainforest, page 118) and also works as a statement plant for kokedama (see page 112) or in a small hanging basket (see Hanging gardens, page 84). It can cope with draughts.

HOW TO GROW

Grow in moist but well-drained, ericaceous compost mixed with a handful of perlite, to improve drainage. Mist plants every few days and feed monthly year-round. Reduce watering in winter. Repot in spring if root-bound.

GROWING TIP

Plants can be divided and potted up individually (see page 31).

Family Pteridaceae

Temperature 5–24°C/41–75°F

Light Bright, indirect light or semi-shade

Water Let the top of the compost feel dry before watering

Height and spread 30x30cm/12x12in

CLASSICAL TOUCH
The genus name *Pellaea* comes from the Greek *pellaios*, which means 'dark' and refers to the stems that turn dark red as they age.

Radiator plant

Peperomia caperata

All *Peperomia* have distinctive leaves and these can be marbled, striped or edged with colour. Radiator plant bears beautiful, corrugated, heart-shaped leaves, and in summer plants send out long, skinny, candlewick flowers. They are easy-going plants to grow.

WHERE TO GROW
Radiator plant appreciates warm humidity so a steamy bathroom is ideal.

HOW TO GROW
Mix a handful of perlite into the compost when planting. Water carefully, avoiding the leaves and crown. Mist daily. In winter, keep the compost almost dry. Feed monthly in spring and summer. Repot only when root-bound.

GROWING TIP
Do not grow radiator plant in too big a pot as it has a shallow root system and struggles if swamped.

Family Piperaceae

Temperature 15–24°C/59–75°F

Light Semi-shade

Water Let the top of the compost dry out before watering in the growing season

Height and spread 25x25cm/10x10in

OTHER NOTABLE SPECIES

- *P. polybotrya* 'Raindrop' (coin leaf peperomia) is a deservedly popular plant with fleshy, teardrop-shaped, green leaves.
- *P. argyreia* (watermelon peperomia) has leaves that are striped dark green and silver and is thus aptly named.

AMONG THE TREES
Just one species from a large genus, these compact, little epiphytes are from the Amazon rainforest.

Simple kokedama

Kokedama is the art of growing plants in a ball of wet soil covered in moss, and it is increasingly popular as an artistic and sculptural way to display plants. It originated as a form of bonsai in Japan and literally translated means 'moss ball'. Plants can be displayed as they are on a saucer or tray, or be hung on twine or wire. The best plants for kokedama are strong architectural and textural ones that are happy in semi- or full shade – direct sunlight will dry out the moss and turn the kokedama brown.

Combine equal amounts of bonsai and multipurpose potting compost to help the ball hold moisture. For the covering, sheet moss is best as it can be gathered around the root ball to make a bag; otherwise, carefully mass together chunks of moss until the ball is smothered in soft green.

To check if the kokedama needs watering, feel the weight of the ball. If it is unnaturally light, leave it to soak in a sink or bucket of water until the compost and moss are saturated; take care not to submerge the leaves. Then let the kokedama drain.

—

PLANTS FOR KOKEDAMA
Asparagus fern (*Asparagus setaceus*)
Coin leaf peperomia (*Peperomia polybotrya* 'Raindrop')
Cretan brake fern (*Pteris cretica*)
Missionary plant (*Pilea peperomioides*)
Staghorn fern (*Platycerium bifurcatum*)

1 Remove the plant (here, *Peperomia polybotrya* 'Raindrop') from its pot and shake off the excess soil from around its roots.

2 Moisten the compost mix until sticky and then compact it into a firm ball around the plant roots until it is about the same size as the plant's original pot.

3 Wrap the ball with moss and then bind it together with twine or florist's wire, winding it around and around the moss ball until it is secure.

4 Tie on a last piece of twine, then hang up the kokedama, out of direct sun.

Heart leaf

Philodendron scandens aka sweetheart plant, love tree

This fast-growing climber has lush, heart-shaped leaves that are very glossy and get bigger and bigger as the plant grows. They are a pretty bronze when young. Also look out for *P. xanadu* with its deeply cut, glossy green leaves.

—

WHERE TO GROW

Heart leaf thrives deep in the rainforest where conditions are humid, warm and dark so replicate this at home — but the lighter the spot the more vigorously it will grow. As it matures, train and support stems against a wall.

HOW TO GROW

Plant in a 2:1 mix of multipurpose compost and perlite. Mist the leaves every few days or grow on a saucer of pebbles and water. Wipe leaves regularly, to clean them. Feed monthly in spring and summer. In winter, water when the top of the compost feels dry.

GROWING TIP

Pinch out the growing tips, to encourage branching and a bushy plant.

Family Araceae

Temperature
16–24°C/61–75°F

Light Bright, indirect light or semi-shade

Water Moist in the growing season

Height and spread
1.5x1.5m/5x5ft

DISPLAY OPTIONS
Heart leaf is often sold supported by a moss pole, but plants will also trail and cascade beautifully, transforming any room into a verdant jungle

Missionary plant

Pilea peperomioides aka Chinese money plant, pancake plant, UFO plant

Hugely popular, these gorgeous little plants have lovely, rounded, fleshy leaves, each with a cute, yellow spot near the centre where the stem meets the leaf. They are neat, compact plants that form loose, handsome domes and are low-maintenance and very easy to grow.

WHERE TO GROW
Display on a windowsill or in the centre of a table – just shelter them from draughts. Plants also make great kokedama feature plants (see Simple kokedama, page 112).

HOW TO GROW
Grow in a 2:1 mix of multipurpose compost and perlite. Mist plants regularly. Feed every couple of weeks in the growing season. Keep the compost just moist in winter, letting the water drain away. Repot in spring when plants are root-bound.

GROWING TIP
Easy to propagate from stem cuttings, in water or potting compost (see page 28–9).

Family Urticaceae

Temperature
15–24°C/59–75°F

Light Bright, indirect light or semi-shade

Water Let the compost dry out before watering in the growing season

Height and spread
30x30cm/12x12in

OTHER NOTABLE SPECIES

- *P. cadierei* (aluminium plant) has blotchy leaves and adds an oomph to terrariums (see Miniature rainforest, page 118) or mixed displays.
- *P. involucrata* (friendship plant) has fuzzy-looking leaves in bronze and green, and loves high humidity.

LATE-COMER
Native to southern China, missionary plants were brought to Europe by a Norwegian missionary in the 1940s. However, being widely unknown by professional growers, its identity was established only in 1984 when an illustration was published in *Kew Magazine*.

Staghorn fern

Platycerium bifurcatum aka elkhorn fern, antelope ears

Staghorn fern is all a house plant should be: easy to grow, magnificent and wonderfully weird. It has two types of fronds: fuzzy fertile ones shaped like a stag's antler; and sterile fronds that are rounder and heart-shaped. The soft down on the fronds protects them against bright light and prevents them from drying out.

WHERE TO GROW
Looks best in a basket or mounted on a chunk of wood or bark, ideally in a steamy room.

HOW TO GROW
Plant in orchid compost. Mist the fertile fronds every day. Water these plants from below (see page 23) if the rounder fronds cover the compost, as these will rot if they get wet. In winter, let the surface of the compost dry out before watering.

GROWING TIP
The flatter, rounder fronds naturally turn brown with age, and new fronds will grow above them.

Family Polypodiaceae

Temperature
10–24°C/50–75°F

Light Bright, indirect light

Water Moist in growing season

Height and spread
30x90cm/12x36in

HELPFUL POINTER
Bifurcatum means 'bifurcated' or 'forked' and refers to the antler-like fertile fronds.

Cretan brake fern

Pteris cretica aka brake fern, ribbon fern, table fern

These are elegant, dainty tropical and subtropical ferns with wiry stems and unusual, ribbon-like leaflets that can be plain green – or striped as with the variegated *P. cretica* var. *albolineata,* which has a broad, central, cream strip.

—

WHERE TO GROW

This is a good plant for the bathroom or kitchen.

HOW TO GROW

Mist every couple of days and place on a tray of wet pebbles, to increase humidity around the plant. Feed monthly in the growing season. Reduce watering slightly through the cooler months; the roots will rot if left sitting in wet compost over winter. Plants are slow-growing but rejuvenate well so tatty fronds can be snipped off at the base. Repot every couple of years.

GROWING TIP

Plants are easily divided (see Propagation by division, page 31), just ensure each piece has at least two fronds and a section of the rhizome.

Family Pteridaceae

Temperature
13–24°C/55–75°F

Light Bright, indirect light or semi-shade

Water Moist in spring and summer

Height and spread
60x60cm/24x24in

DIRECT HEAT
Keep Cretan brake fern away from hot radiators and out of bright sun, which will scorch its leaves.

Miniature rainforest

Terrariums are a lovely way to display plants, creating a tiny garden within its own miniature glass world. Tropical rainforest plants that dislike direct light are perfect for such planters as they thrive in the humid environment that the sealed glass helps to create. Small ferns such as button fern, delta maidenhair fern and Cretan brake fern introduce a range of leaf shapes, while plants such as mosaic plant, polka dot plant and aluminium plant have pretty spots or stripes.

You can use specialist terrariums, but scrupulously clean glass jars, vases, bottles or aquariums work well, too. However, bottles and anything with a narrow neck are tricky to plant so use long tools such as spoons, dibbers and chopsticks to help you. Grit or gravel mixed with activated charcoal helps with drainage and air movement within the terrarium, as well as stopping the growth of fungi.

Plants in a terrarium require misting frequently, to maintain the humid environment. However, they need less water than traditionally potted plants – check the surface of the compost regularly and, when dry, water with a can fitted with a rose.

—

PLANTS FOR A MINIATURE RAINFOREST
Aluminium plant (*Pilea cadierei*)
Bird's nest fern (*Asplenium nidus* and *A.n.* 'Parvati')
Button fern (*Pellaea rotundifolia*)
Cretan brake fern (*Pteris cretica*)
Delta maidenhair fern (*Adiantum raddianum*)
Mosaic plant (*Fittonia albivenis*)
Polka dot plant (*Hypoestes phyllostachya*)

1. Add a layer of grit or gravel and activated charcoal to the base of the terrarium and then cover with 5–7cm/2–3in compost.
2. Remove each plant (here Cretan brake fern, mosaic plant and *Asplenium nidus* 'Parvati') from its pot and place in the compost, filling in and firming down where needed.
3. Cover the compost with a generous layer of moss or decorative pebbles. This will help to maintain humidity levels within the terrarium and set off the plants well.
4. Wipe the glass clean both inside and out, then place the terrarium in a bright spot, but not in direct sunlight, which will scorch the plants through the glass.

Bamboo palm

Rhapsis excelsa aka lady palm, broadleaf lady palm

The unusual, bamboo-like stems and broad, blunt leaves are quite different to those on a typical palm. Bamboo palms are dramatic, bushy plants, ideal for first-time or nervous growers who want to make a statement.

—

WHERE TO GROW
Being happy in low light, bamboo plant will add interest to a dead corner or hallway. It is slow-growing, too, so although plants eventually get very large most reach only 2m/7ft.

HOW TO GROW
Plant in a 3:1 mix of soil-based potting compost and perlite. Mist the leaves once a week in summer, to keep them fresh. Ensure the compost is evenly moist but not sodden, as roots will rot if kept too wet, particularly in winter. Feed two or three times in the growing season. Repot plants only when root-bound.

GROWING TIP
Offshoots can be divided from the base and potted on into new plants (see Propagation by offsets, page 31).

Family	Arecaceae
Temperature	5–25°C/41–77°F
Light	Semi-shade/shade
Water	Moist
Height and spread	3x2m/10x7ft

ENDANGERED
Bamboo palm is believed to be native to southern China, but there are no longer any known plants left in the wild and they exist only in cultivation.

Mistletoe cactus

Rhipsalis baccifera

Unlike its more predictable cacti cousins, mistletoe cactus is spineless and prefers humidity and dimmer rather than bright light. Its common name comes from its white berries, which may follow cream, white or yellow flowers that appear in summer when plants are mature.

WHERE TO GROW
This weeping epiphytic cactus is perfect for a hanging basket (see Hanging gardens, page 84) or kokedama (see Simple Kokedama, page 112) in a warm bathroom, where it will cascade shaggily.

HOW TO GROW
Increase humidity by misting every few days. Water well in the growing season, but ease off in winter, unless the plant is in a very hot room. Mistletoe cactus can tolerate drought, but its stems will start to shrivel. Feed once a month in the growing season.

GROWING TIP
Stem cuttings root easily if they are left to callus over and then planted in moist compost (see pages 28–9).

Family Cactaceae

Temperature
15–29°C/59–84°F

Light Semi-shade/shade

Water Let top of compost dry out between watering

Height and spread
90x60cm/36x24in

FAR-REACHING
Mistletoe cactus is the only cactus found in the old and new world – intriguingly it is at home in both tropical America and Africa and in Sri Lanka, and theories abound, including dispersal by sailors and birds, as to how this can be!

African violet

Saintpaulia cultivars

These pretty plants have been firm favourites as house plants for a long time, thanks to their soft, fuzzy leaves and small flowers in purple, pink, white or red. Blooms can also be frilly, two-tone, single or double; if happy, plants flower almost continuously.

WHERE TO GROW

Such small, low-growing plants are ideal for a windowsill or shelf out of a draught. During the growing season, an east- or west-facing spot is perfect; in winter, move to a south-facing window.

HOW TO GROW

Plants appreciate humidity so grow on or next to a tray of wet pebbles. Protect the leaves by watering plants from below (see page 23) with tepid water; avoid cold water as it can mark and damage leaves. Feed once a month in the growing season. Deadhead fading flowers regularly. Repot plants every two to three years, in spring.

GROWING TIP

Plants can be propagated very easily from leaf cuttings, rooting in both water or compost (see page 28), as well as from stem cuttings (see page 28–9).

Family Gesneriaceae	
Temperature 16–24°C/61–75°F	
Light Bright, indirect light	
Water Let the top of the compost dry out before watering	
Height and spread 10x20cm/4x8in	

HABITAT CRISIS
Most of the many cultivars available are from *S. ionantha*, which sadly is now classified as near threatened in the wild due to its natural habitat being cleared for agriculture.

Snake plant

Sansevieria trifasciata aka mother-in-law's tongue, good luck plant, devil's tongue

A house plant classic that grows slowly and lasts for many years, snake plant produces clusters of tough, silvery green, sword-like leaves in dense rosettes and is tolerant of erratic watering and extremes of light conditions.

—

WHERE TO GROW

It is one of the best plants for purifying the air (see Natural air fresheners, page 124) so position in a bedroom or living room.

HOW TO GROW

Plant into a free-draining cactus compost mix (see Cacti and succulents, page 22) and a pot that is not too big – snake plant likes its roots crowded so choose one that is a snug fit. Feed once a month from spring to autumn. In winter, reduce watering to just once a month. Repot only when plants are tightly root-bound.

GROWING TIP

Plants are easily propagated by leaf cuttings (see page 28) or by division (see page 31), teasing away new stems that are growing around the base of the plant.

Family Asparagaceae

Temperature
15–24°C/59–75°F

Light Semi-shade

Water Let the top of the compost dry out before watering in the growing season

Height and spread
75x30cm/30x12in

MULTI-GENERATION
These are plants that are handed down in families and are well-loved for their forgiving and easy-going nature.

OTHER NOTABLE SPECIES

- *S. cylindrica* (African spear) is a stunning plant with long, slim, cylindrical leaves. It is very drought-tolerant and only needs watering every couple of weeks through the growing season.
- *S. trifasciata* var. *laurentii* has striking, yellow-edged leaves; this is probably the most popular house plant.
- *S. zeylanica* is less well known than *S. trifasciata*, but is similarly tough, with silver-and-green-mottled leaves and stripes of darker green.

Sansevieria zeylanica

Natural air fresheners

Studies have shown that many house plants can boost physical health and well-being by improving the air quality in our homes. Their leaves and stems soak up the harmful toxins and chemicals such as formaldehyde, xylene and benzene found in plastics, household detergents, paints, varnishes, carpets and furniture, and thereby leave the atmosphere cleaner. When grouped together, the effect of any of the following plants will be even stronger than when positioned individually. Living rooms and bedrooms are good spots to grow these plants, but, if you choose the right ones and scatter them in every room, your whole house can benefit.

To ensure that leaves effectively absorb harmful particles, keep them clean and dust-free.

—

PLANTS THAT IMPROVE AIR QUALITY

Bamboo palm (*Rhapis excelsa*)
Bellmore sentry palm (*Howea forsteriana*)
Bird's nest fern (*Asplenium nidus*)
Boston fern (*Nephrolepis exaltata*)
Cast-iron plant (*Aspidistra elatior*)
Delta maidenhair fern (*Adiantum raddianum*)
Dumb cane (*Dieffenbachia seguine*)
Fiddle-leaf fig (*Ficus lyrata*)
Goeppertia 'Whitestar'
Jade plant (*Crassula ovata*)
Mother-in-law's tongue (*Sansevieria zeylanica*)
Peace lily (*Spathiphyllum wallisii* 'Bellini')
Rubber plant (*Ficus elastica*)
Snake plant (*Sansevieria trifasciata*)
Spider plant (*Chlorophytum comosum* 'Variegatum')

1

2

3

4

1 Use a soft cloth to wipe the dust from larger-leaved plants (here, fiddle-leaf fig).

2 Check grouped plants individually, and water each according to its needs.

3/4 To remove ammonia, benzene, formaldehyde and xylene from the atmosphere, grow spider plants (here, *Chlorophytum comosum* 'Ocean') or larger-leaved cultivars (here, *Asplenium nidus* 'Crispy Wave').

5 If any gets too big for the display, move it to another home and swap with something new.

5

North American pitcher plant

Sarracenia flava aka trumpet pitchers, pitcher plant, huntsman's horns

The North American pitcher plant belongs to a small genus of carnivorous plants whose long, colourful leaves have evolved into striking pitchers to trap insects. These each have a strong-smelling nectar around the neck, which draws prey to and into the pitcher from which insects cannot escape.

—

Family Sarraceniaceae

Temperature −5–25°C/23–77°F

Light Sunny

Water Wet in spring and summer

Height and spread 30x15cm/12x6in

WHERE TO GROW

Thrives on a windowsill in a bright room; although tolerant of a little shade, it is happier in bright, direct light. In autumn, move your plant to a cooler room, just 10°C/50°F or less, until early spring.

HOW TO GROW

Grow North American pitcher plant in a specialist carnivorous plant mix (see page 22). Stand on a tray of rain- or distilled water in spring and summer; in autumn, remove the tray but keep the compost just moist. When dormant, leaves die back but resist the urge to tidy them until they turn papery brown in winter. In summer, you can put plants outdoors, to catch insect prey; they do not need feeding (see also Carnivorous vase, page 68).

GROWING TIP

Repot in autumn only when plants are quite root-bound, as North American pitcher plant prefers to be snug about the roots.

EXOTIC TOUCH
Pitchers come in shades of lime, burgundy, red and pink and are often mottled or veined and have wonderful, slightly space-age flowers that match the colour of the pitchers.

OTHER NOTABLE SPECIES

- *S.* x *mitcheliana* 'Bella' is a beautiful hybrid with red, white and pink veining on the lids and pitchers, and scarlet flowers in spring.
- *S. psittacina* (parrot pitcher) has horizontal pitchers that are veined red, white or green; they catch crawling insects and even tadpoles when it is completely submerged in its native wetlands.
- *S. purpurea* subsp. *purpurea* has squat pitchers flushed with burgundy and produces purplish red flowers in spring.

Dwarf umbrella tree

Schefflera arboricola aka parasol plant

These stately, handsome plants produce glossy, evergreen, hand-shaped leaves on tall stems. They are tough, forgiving plants that cope comfortably with central heating. Many variegated varieties are available with yellow, cream or gold markings, such as *S. arboricola* 'Gold Capella'.

—

WHERE TO GROW
Although dwarf umbrella tree tolerates poor light and erratic watering, it will thrive in a warm room out of direct sun and draughts. Keep away from pets and children, as all parts are toxic.

HOW TO GROW
Give dwarf umbrella tree a heavy pot to stop it toppling over. Water well in the growing season, allowing the water to drain through the pot. Mist weekly or place on a tray of wet pebbles. Feed monthly in the growing season, and wipe leaves to keep them glossy and dust-free (see Natural air fresheners, page 124). Reduce watering in winter, to just once a month. Repot plants every couple of years in spring.

GROWING TIP
If leaves turn yellow and fall from the plant, it is being overwatered. Reduce watering, so the compost is no longer soggy.

Family Araliaceae

Temperature
15–24°C/59–75°F

Light Bright, indirect light or semi-shade

Water Allow the top of the compost to dry out before watering

Height and spread
2.5x1m/8x3ft

INDIGENOUS PLANTS
In the wild, plants have clusters of nectar-rich, red flowers in summer, followed by rounded orange fruits, but unfortunately plants rarely flower indoors

Christmas cactus

Schlumbergera x buckleyi aka holiday cactus, crab claw cactus, Thanksgiving cactus

The perfect winter gift, this tropical cactus has flat, prettily segmented, trailing stems and is tipped in neon-pink flowers in winter. Plants are easy to grow and cope well with neglect, but if you want further flowers they do need a little more care.

—

WHERE TO GROW

Sturdy, young bushes develop weeping stems as they mature and these look lovely in baskets or trailing over a shelf. For best results, position away from draughts and radiators.

HOW TO GROW

Grow in a gritty compost mix (see Cacti and succulents, page 22). Mist plants every day or place on a saucer of wet pebbles. Feed once a month from mid-spring to early autumn. In mid-autumn, reduce watering to promote flowering. When buds appear in midwinter, resume watering. After flowering, stop watering for a few more weeks. Repot in spring only when plants are root-bound. Shape plants by pinching off stem segments in spring.

GROWING TIP

To promote flowering, move plants to a cool room in early autumn and give them total darkness for twelve hours a day until buds appear after 6–8 weeks.

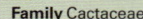

Family Cactaceae

Temperature
12–27°C/54–80°F

Light Bright, indirect light

Water Moist from spring to early autumn

Height and spread
45x45cm/18x18in

SEASONAL COLOUR
The Christmas cactus is a hybrid of *S. russelliana* and *S. truncata* and was originally crossed by William Buckley of Rollisson Nurseries in the 1840s. There are now many varieties in red, mauve, yellow and orange.

Donkey's tail

Sedum morganianum aka burro' tail, lamb's tail, horse's tail

These stonecrops are hugely desirable with their long, trailing stems covered in plump, dusty green and blue leaves. They are one of the best succulents for drawing the eye and, if you are lucky, rosy pink flowers will bloom at the tips of the 'tails' in summer.

—

WHERE TO GROW
Plant in a mix of two parts cactus compost and one part grit. Donkey's tail is a great focal point, whether grown in a hanging basket or trailing over a shelf or windowsill. It needs a warm, bright spot in full sun to thrive, and bright, direct light will help to encourage flowering.

HOW TO GROW
Plants can get heavy as they get older and longer, so give each a sturdy pot. Feed monthly in the growing season. From late autumn, water plants just once a month. Repot plants when root-bound, every two or three years, in spring.

GROWING TIP
Handle plants carefully as the fleshy leaves break off with the slightest nudge, but they will root easily if laid on top of compost to make new plants (see Propagation by adventitious roots, page 32).

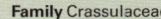

Family Crassulaceae

Temperature
10–27°C/50–80°F

Light Sun or bright light

Water Let the top of the compost dry out before watering in the growing season

Height and spread
10x60cm/4x24in

DETECTIVE WORK
Despite being in cultivation since 1935, donkey's tail was one of just a few cultivated plants whose habitat in the wild was unknown. Finally, after years of searching it was spotted in 2010 growing in remote ravines in Veracruz, Mexico.

Peace lily

Spathiphyllum wallisii aka white sails, spathe flower

Stylish plants, these have glossy, green leaves and an elegant, open habit. They are easy to look after and, considering their boggy homes in the wild, very forgiving of neglect. Their flowers cluster on a spike, or spadix, which is surrounded by a spathe – a pure white 'petal', which fades to green and lasts for several weeks.

—

WHERE TO GROW

Although tolerant of very low light levels, peace lily prefers brighter conditions, particularly if you want it to flower. A bathroom is a good choice as plants are adept at removing mould spores from the air (see Natural air fresheners, page 124).

HOW TO GROW

Mist plants often and grow on a tray of damp pebbles, to keep humidity levels high. Dust the shiny leaves regularly. Snip off fading flower stems and any yellow leaves. Feed plants once in summer. In winter, water only when the top of the compost has dried out. Repot in spring, in a pot just one size up as peace lily prefers life a little snug.

GROWING TIP

Plants do not like tap water, particularly in hard water areas. Therefore, collect rainwater or leave tap water to stand for a few hours before using, so that the chlorine can evaporate.

Family Araceae

Temperature
12–24°C/54–75°F

Light Bright, indirect light and semi-shade

Water Moist in the growing season

Height and spread
60x60cm/24x24in

NO RELATIVE
Peace lilies are not true lilies and instead are in the same family as dumb cane (see page 61) and heart leaf (see page 114).

Stephanotis

Stephanotis floribunda aka Madagascar jasmine, bridal wreath

These glorious, twining climbers are a visual and sensory delight. They produce shiny, green leaves and long-lasting, fragrant, white flowers in summer.

WHERE TO GROW

In flower this is a showstopper whose fragrance will fill a room, so give it pride of place in a sunny spot; keep it away from draughts. It can be trained up and across a wall, or around supports such as a hoop if you have less room. Move to a cooler area, 18°C/64°F, in winter.

HOW TO GROW

Mist regularly, especially in summer, and place on a tray of damp pebbles. Give high-potash feed every couple of weeks from spring to autumn. In winter, allow the top of the compost to dry out before watering. Plants can be trimmed in spring, to keep them in shape.

GROWING TIP

Plants prefer life slightly root-bound so repot every three years; or replace the top layer of compost each spring.

Family Apocynaceae

Temperature
10–23°C/50–73°F

Light Bright, indirect light

Water Moist in the growing season

Height and spread
3x3m/10x10ft

GOOD LUCK TOKEN
The pretty, trumpet-shaped flowers with their jasmine-like scent are a traditional flower in bridal bouquets.

Driftwood anchor

Air plants are fascinating plants that have no roots and can survive happily in the wild without soil and very little water. They are, therefore, extremely easy to look after and can be used in the house in all sorts of ways – placed in pretty shells, jars or bowls or attached to foraged pieces of bark or attractive branches and hung up or placed on tables, shelves or windowsills out of direct sun. Driftwood collected from the beach complements the glaucous leaves of air plants well but must be submerged in clean water for a couple of weeks before using it to remove any salt residue in the wood.

Having arranged the air plants across your piece of bark or wood, you can either leave them loose or secure them in place by tying them gently with florist's wire, thread or fishing line. Do not be tempted to use glue, which will damage the plants.

Mist air plants twice a week, preferably with rainwater, to keep the humidity levels around the plants high, and untie them once a week so they can be soaked in tepid rainwater.

—

GOOD AIR PLANTS FOR DISPLAY
Tillandsia argentea
T. brachycaulos var. *multiflora*
T. capitata 'Peach'
T. usneoides
T. xerographica

1

2

3

1 Assemble your air plants (here, *Tillandsia*), some well-soaked driftwood, a roll of florist's wire and scissors.
2 Before 'planting', soak plants for a few minutes in a sink filled with tepid rather than cold rainwater. Then stand them upside down on a soft cloth so that excess water can drain away.
3 Secure plants in place by tying florist's wire loosely around the main body of each plant.
4 Place your air-plant branch in a humid spot out of direct sun.

4

Cape primrose

Streptocarpus hybrids

These house plants have a long flowering season, from spring to autumn, and are easy to care for, springing back brilliantly from neglect, even when their leaves are wilting.

WHERE TO GROW
Give them a home on an east- or west-facing windowsill.

HOW TO GROW
Water plants either from below (see page 23) or from above (see page 23), but always allow plants to drain well afterwards as the roots can easily rot. Feed once a month from spring to autumn, but do not overfeed, or overwater, which will produce plenty of leafy growth but no flowers. Deadhead flower stems as the blooms fade. In winter, Cape primrose can sit almost dry – plants recover very well from dehydration. Nip out old leaves in spring, to make room for fresh growth.

GROWING TIP
Cape primrose likes to feel slightly constricted so always give it a small pot, even when potting it up in spring.

Family Gesneriaceae

Temperature 12–24°C/54–75°F

Light Bright, indirect light or semi-shade

Water Allow the top of the compost to dry out before watering in the growing season

Height and spread 60x60cm/24x24in

OTHER NOTABLE HYBRIDS

- *S.* 'Delia' has white flowers with subtle blue veins on the lower petals.
- *S.* 'Harlequin Blue' is a stunning, two-tone variety with lemon-yellow lower lobes, bright blue upper petals and a deep purple-lined throat. Plants are neat and compact.
- *S.* 'Hope' has vibrant pink blooms with a flash of yellow in the throat and white on the upper petals.
- *S.* 'Kim' forms compact plants that flower early, with dramatic, inky blue flowers.
- *S.* 'Polka-Dot Purple' is a prolific flowerer with striking, white-and-purple-mottled blooms.

Air plant
Tillandsia species

The ultimate easy-care plant, these delightful little bromeliads need no soil to grow in, hence their name; and they survive on very little water and attention. Air plants come in all sorts of forms and sizes – some are dense and sprawling, others spidery and spiky. Many will flower colourfully in the growing season, once mature; they then die, having also produced baby plants to replace themselves.

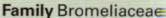

Family Bromeliaceae	
Temperature 15–24°C/59–75°F	
Light Bright, indirect light	
Water Soak once a week	
Height and spread 10x45cm/4x18in	

WHERE TO GROW
Air plants are happiest in a humid spot, such as a bathroom or kitchen, out of draughts and away from radiators or fires. They can be displayed hanging from driftwood or bark or in jars or shells, but resist the temptation to use glue to attach them (see also Driftwood anchor, page 134).

HOW TO GROW
Soak plants in a bowl of tepid rain- or distilled water. Make sure they dry by draining well or hanging upside down, as excess water causes rotting. Do not wet the flowers.

GROWING TIP
Standing an air plant in the neck of a jar of water will give it the humidity it craves and is also an interesting, easy way to display it.

HABITAT RANGE
Many air plants are typical epiphytes, living on other plants, either hanging from branches or nestled among tree trunks, but some are aerophytes and have no roots at all, growing on unstable desert sands.

NOTABLE SPECIES
- *T. argentea* has thin, spidery leaves that radiate from a central bulb and produces striking, red and purple flower heads.
- *T. bulbosa* is eye-catching, with its spiral of twisted leaves, long, sculptural shape and pink and purple flowers in spring.
- *T. cyanea* bears an oval flower head comprising bright pink bracts and purple flowers.
- *T. usneoides* (Spanish moss) produces bundles of delicate, curly leaves, which work well hanging from a pot or hook.
- *T. xerographica* is the largest and most striking air plant you will probably find; it has thick, silvery leaves that curl into a dense clump.

Silver-inch plant

Tradescantia zebrina aka spiderwort, wandering Jew

The striped, zebra-like pattern on the fleshy leaves has given this attractive plant its common name. The undersides are purple, as are the young leaves, so plants actually have a decorative, multicoloured look. They also bear lovely, three-petalled, lavender flowers.

—

WHERE TO GROW

An east- or west-facing window in a hanging basket or tumbling over a shelf or windowsill is perfect. Plants will revert to green if light levels drop too low.

HOW TO GROW

Grow in a free-draining mix of 3:1 potting compost and perlite. Mist plants weekly in spring and summer, and feed monthly also. The fleshy leaves can withstand drought for a while, but growth will be halted until watering resumes. In winter, reduce watering so that compost is kept just moist. Trim stems in spring, to encourage bushy growth. Cut plants right back if they become neglected and tatty. Repot plants only when root-bound.

GROWING TIP

Plants can be propagated very easily from leaf cuttings rooted in water or compost (see page 28).

NEW WORLD FIND
The botanists John Tradescant the Elder (1570–1638) and his son John Tradescant the Younger (1608–1662) brought *Tradescantia virginiana* back from a collecting trip to Virginia in North America.

Family Commelinaceae

Temperature
12–24°C/54–75°F

Light Bright, indirect light

Water Allow the top of the compost to almost dry out before watering in the growing season

Height and spread
15x60cm/6x24in

Spineless yukka
Yucca elephantipes aka stick yukka

The perfect statement plant, these architectural showstoppers are tough, tolerant of drought and love sunbathing in direct light. Each palm-like trunk has a tuft of sword-shaped leaves sprouting from the top. If happy, a mature plant may bear spikes of scented, creamy white flowers in summer and autumn.

—

WHERE TO GROW
Spineless yukka thrives when basking in front of a south-facing window.

HOW TO GROW
Feed monthly in the growing season. In winter, water plants just once a month. Repot every two years or, if repotting a large plant is tricky, freshen the top layer of compost.

GROWING TIP
If spineless yukka gets too tall, simply cut its trunk with a saw in spring; new leaves will soon appear.

Family Asparagaceae

Temperature
10–27˚C/50–80˚F

Light Sun or bright, indirect light

Water Allow the top of the compost to dry out between watering in the growing season

Height and spread
1.5x0.75m/5x2½ft

CULINARY TREAT
Many parts of yukka are useful or edible. In El Salvador, where they are the national flower, the flowers (*Flor de Izote*) are traditionally eaten with scrambled eggs and tacos.

Fern arum

Zamioculcas zamiifolia aka ZZ plant, Zanzibar gem, zuzu plant

The handsome, glossy foliage of this plant is known as ladders after the leaf pairs that are borne along its upright stems. Slow-growing and easy to look after, fern arum is happy in both sun and shade and even tolerates the odd missed watering, so is ideal for nervous and first-time growers.

—

WHERE TO GROW
It is very effective at purifying the air (see Natural air fresheners, page 124) so a warm bedroom or living room in a north-facing window is a good choice.

HOW TO GROW
Plants have succulent, fleshy rhizomes that help them withstand drought, but if kept dry plants will become dormant, look far less handsome and eventually start to drop their leaves. Feed monthly from spring to autumn. Water plants just once a month in winter. Trim plants if they need to be kept in shape, in spring. Repot plants every two years.

GROWING TIP
Yellow leaves are a sure sign that plants are being overwatered.

Family Araceae

Temperature
15–24°C/59–75°F

Light Bright, indirect light or semi-shade

Water Allow the top of the compost to dry out between watering in the growing season

Height and spread
75x60cm/30x24in

RECENT ARRIVAL
New to the house plant scene, fern arum was first commercially cultivated as recently as 1996 by Dutch nurseries.

Index

Brimming with creative inspiration, how-to projects and useful information to enrich your everyday life, Quarto Knows is a favourite destination for those pursuing their interests and passions. Visit our site and dig deeper with our books into your area of interest:Quarto Creates, Quarto Cooks, Quarto Homes, Quarto Lives, Quarto Drives, Quarto Explores, Quarto Gifts, or Quarto Kids.

First published in 2019 by White Lion Publishing,
an imprint of The Quarto Group.
The Old Brewery, 6 Blundell Street
London, N7 9BH,
United Kingdom
T (0)20 7700 6700 F (0)20 7700 8066
www.QuartoKnows.com

Text © 2019 Kay Maguire
Project photographs © 2019 Jason Ingram
Illustrations © the Board of Trustees of the Royal Botanic Gardens, Kew, unless otherwise stated

ISBN 978-0-7112-4000-1

10 9 8 7 6 5 4 3 2 1

Typeset in Stempel Garamond and Univers
Design by Glenn Howard

Printed in China

Picture acknowledgements
t=top; b=below; m=middle; l=left; r=right

© Alamy Stock Photo: 33 Avalon/Photoshot License, 78l Fir Mamat, 101r Universal Images Group North America LLC/DeAgostini, 108l Universal Images Group North America LLC/DeAgostini, 129 blickwinkel/tomcook

© Bolus Herbarium, University of Cape Town 80r

Courtesy of the Carnegie Institution for Science: 104r

By kind permission of the Barbara Everard Gallery/ the Barbara Everard Trust for Orchid Conservation (www.barbara-everard.com): 90, 131

© Jason Ingram: 41, 51, 63, 69, 75, 85, 97, 107, 113, 119, 125, 135

© DeAgostini/Getty Images: 110

Reprinted with permission from The New York Botanical Garden: 47

© SANBI: (Haworthia fasciata, G. Condy) 86, (Senecio rowleyanus, G. Condy) 92

© Shutterstock: 2 fneun, 6–7 Followtheflow, 8 TY Lim, 11 CLICKMANIS, 12l sirtravelalot, 12tr Todd Boland, 12br Vadim Lavra, 14 sundaemorning, 15t Loveandrock, 15bl Maslov Dmitry, 15br CK2 Connect Studio, 17 WitchitS, 18t rattiya lamrod, 18m Chapatta, 18b funkyfrogstock, 19 haveseen, 21 panattar, 23 Apple_Mac, 25 brizmaker, 26t nito, 26m Yayuyu2105, 26b victorias, 27 Marianna Karabut, 29 Yauheniya Stryzhak, 30 jelloyd, 32 sasimoto, 34–5 rattiya lamrod, 37l Real Moment, 38l Sally Wallis, 42l Boibin, 44l Anna Greben, 47l cctm, 53bl Bozhena Melnyk, 54l BPP Mecca, 57l Bozhena Melnyk, 59l Junsang N, 60l New Africa, 61l giedre vaitekune, 64l Robert Anaya Jr, 65l ma_ylooo, 67l Yongxi, 73l Niney Azman, 76l Ekkamai Chaikata, 78r Shelsea Forward, 79l Alina Kuptsova, 80l Ian Grainger, 81l Transient Eternal, 82l Voravuth sompaiboon, 83l Young Swee Ming, 88l Oana Raluca, 90l sima nusume, 95l sharohyip, 99tl aimpol buranet, 99b Supaleka_P, 100l rattiya lamrod, 100r Ratchanee Swasdijir , 101l Podolnaya Elena, 103l Tatyana Abramovich, 104l Phawat, 105l Saturn29, 111l Supaleka_P, 114l atupong Arsaipanit, 114r Abdecoral, 116l ChaiyonS021 116r senee sriyota, 117l ekapol sirachainan, 120l M imagine, 121l Prispim, 126l Del Boy, 128l Michal Ludwiczak, 128r Remzi, 130l Nadezhda Nesterova, 131l ja avenue, 132l armifello, 133l Totokzww, 136 Konstantin Gushcha, 140l Alexeysun, 140r kirillov alexey, 141l celiachen

The publishers wish to thank Martyn Rix and the Kew Library Art and Archives team, and Marcelo Sellaro.